# LEADING through LOSS

## HOW TO NAVIGATE GRIEF AT WORK

### MARGO M. FOWKES

Find Your Harbor Press

Margo Fowkes works with leaders to create more compassionate cultures by acknowledging and addressing grief and loss in the workplace.

To learn more, visit:
www.ontargetconsulting.net

# More Praise for *Leading Through Loss*

"*Leading Through Loss* has some very practical applications for leading employees during times of grief, for both the employee experiencing the loss and the colleagues surrounding them. Leaders would do well to take this book and apply it broadly across employees' experiences of grief, including loss of loved ones to death, severe illness, estrangement, and prison."

—Stephanie Baldwin, Vice President,
  Airport Operations, Delta Air Lines

"*Leading Through Loss* is a truly thoughtful and illuminating guide to conceptualizing and addressing grief and loss in the workplace. Anyone who has struggled with what to say to or how to support a grieving colleague can benefit from this book. I highly recommend this resource for both corporate and nonprofit leaders."

—Mark Schuster, founding dean and CEO,
  Kaiser Permanente Bernard J. Tyson School of
  Medicine

"Margo Fowkes's extraordinary book brings to light the prevalence of grief in the workplace, its impact on organizations of all types, and the drain it causes on creativity, engagement, and profitability. But thankfully, Margo gives us a new toolbox that is filled with methods and practices we can use to support those who are navigating their grief at work."

—David Woods Bartley, TEDx speaker and
  international mental health educator

*For Jimmy, whose curiosity and kindness inspire me still*

*For Dan and Molly, who made living on possible*

* * *

Leadership is not about being in charge.
Leadership is about taking care of those in
your charge.

—Simon Sinek

# Contents

# Facing the Challenge of Grief at Work

> There were people who didn't know how to react to the death of my son. That was awkward because I had to make them feel comfortable. They wanted to say something, but they didn't know what to say, and they were afraid I was going to cry. So they didn't say anything at all.
>
> —Linda Knight Crane

GRIEF IS AN INESCAPABLE PART of life. The death of one or more of our essential people will knock us sideways, often in unexpected ways, and when it happens, we will bring our pain and sadness into work with us. Yet the vast majority of workplaces are ill-prepared to navigate the minefield of loss.

Regardless of how and when grief shows up in your workplace (and it will, if it hasn't already), this book can help you navigate it.

*Leading Through Loss* offers practical tools and ideas from leaders who've dealt with loss, either their own or that of their employees, and provides insight into the perspectives and experiences of grieving employees: what they want and need, what helps and what hurts, what support they were deeply grateful for, and what they wish their leaders had done differently.

The twenty-five leaders who were interviewed for the book span all levels from manager to CEO. They work in a wide variety of industries—from manufacturing to nonprofits, high school to high tech. In the chapters that follow, they describe the mistakes they've made, share their hard-won wisdom, and offer advice in their own words.

*Leading Through Loss* provides the information you need to create a compassionate culture in your workplace, which goes well beyond offering bereavement leave. The vast majority of US companies provide just three days of paid time off after the death of an employee's loved one, which isn't enough time to handle the funeral arrangements, deal with the initial legal and financial issues, and obtain a death certificate, much less grieve.

In 2017, two years after the death of her husband, Survey-Monkey CEO David Goldberg, Sheryl Sandberg announced that Facebook employees would now receive up to twenty days of paid leave to grieve a member of their immediate family and up to ten days to grieve an extended family member. She called on other companies to do the same, but only SurveyMonkey and Mastercard followed suit.

While having two weeks or a month of bereavement leave, instead of a few days, is undoubtedly beneficial, the CEOs, senior leaders, and other bereaved employees interviewed for this book were unequivocal that what matters far more is whether the team and the organization acknowledge the loss and how the manager and the rest of the team handle a grieving employee's return to work.

If an employee has a heart attack, they will be on leave for four to twelve weeks and return with a reduced or adjusted workload and other accommodations. Their coworkers will send cards and flowers, drop off meals, and cover their assignments until they recover. People will ask how they're feeling, express concern, and offer to take work off of their plate.

But if that same employee's child dies, they will likely be allotted just three or four days of bereavement leave. Their manager and a handful of coworkers might send a note, drop off a meal, or attend the memorial service. When the grieving parent returns to work, the assignments that piled up while they were gone will probably be waiting for them. A few people might ask if they're "okay," but most will feel awkward or uncomfortable and opt to say nothing at all. Even the brave souls willing to bring up their deceased child will stop asking or offering extra assistance within a few weeks or months. Team members may wonder why the grieving employee doesn't smile as easily as they used to or notice that their colleague has gotten quieter in meetings, but no one will ask.

When the grieving employee misses a deadline or makes a mistake, their coworkers will feel frustrated. Even if they consider that grief could be the cause, they may not check in or find out where and how the grieving person is struggling. When the silence and lack of understanding forces the employee to do their best to return to their old self or stop mentioning their child, their colleagues will assume they're over their grief.

Finding ways to support someone who's grieving is challenging under any circumstances but particularly in the workplace. Death can happen without warning, leaving leaders unprepared and unsure of what to do beyond what's in the employee handbook—a few days of bereavement leave, an employee assistance plan or program (EAP), and access to counseling or a grief group. An effective, compassionate response requires forethought and planning. Ignoring a colleague's loss can be costly as unaddressed, unacknowledged grief will take a physical, mental, and emotional toll on an employee, a team, and the workplace as a whole.

This book will help you successfully navigate the murky, sometimes treacherous waters of grief in the workplace by:

- unpacking the varied and complex experience of grief
- outlining what it will cost you, your team, and your organization if you fail to address an employee's grief
- demystifying how to acknowledge an employee's loss and educate the rest of the team on how to support their grieving colleague
- advising you on how to create a plan that will allow the grieving employee to return to work feeling supported
- detailing the actions that need to be taken when an employee dies and offering ideas on how to honor the loss in a meaningful way
- providing a road map on how to navigate your own grief while you continue to lead the team or organization
- specifying ways to support a grieving employee in a virtual or hybrid workplace

As consultant Alan Weiss says, we don't have a personal life and a work life; we have a life. Coworkers can become some of our closest friends. After a death, the workplace can be a distraction, a source of comfort, even a haven where we can cope with our grief and begin to heal. Death is both universal and unavoidable, and grief is the natural response when we lose someone dear to us. It's time we got better at supporting each other through it, especially in the workplace.

Most managers have good intentions, but without firsthand experience with devastating loss, they are left confused and confounded as to how to support someone who has just suffered one.

Their awkward efforts, no matter how well-meaning, can cause lasting damage to their relationships with their colleagues and to the morale and health of the organization.

While no one can plan for every contingency or anticipate every tragedy, organizations and their leaders need to be ready to offer more than a few days of leave and access to counseling. Robust, clearly defined bereavement policies and a willingness to have frequent, open conversations about grief and loss will enable you and your leadership team to face and navigate a broad range of difficult situations. Successfully supporting bereaved employees at every level, including the CEO, requires brave leaders who will acknowledge the presence of grief in the workplace and a compassionate culture in which grieving employees are both seen and supported over an extended period of time.

# 1

# Understanding the Impact of Grief in the Workplace

I began asking people how they found the return to work. Everybody had the same answer, which was 'I never wanted to do it, and I didn't have any choice. I didn't have any support, so I just kind of got on with it.' I thought, *That's so rubbish*. Surely, there's a better way for us to be talking about this.

— Lucy Dennis

FEBRUARY 5, 2011, BEGAN LIKE any other Saturday for Delta Air Lines fleet manager Tim Moye: a round of golf, followed by a relaxing afternoon at home watching golf on TV. The house was quiet. Tim's youngest son, Jason, was working out of town as a welder assistant on a pipeline. Tim's wife and Jason's fiancée were out shopping for the wedding. Tim had been trying to reach Jason all day without success, so when the phone rang, he expected to hear his youngest son's voice. Instead, a police officer informed him that Jason had been found dead in his hotel room. In an instant, Tim went from planning his twenty-five-year-old son's wedding to arranging his funeral.

Tim's manager told him to take all the time he needed before returning to work. His team did whatever they could to be supportive—sending notes of condolence, attending the viewing and funeral, covering Tim's work to be sure he didn't fall behind. But none of his colleagues had lost a child, and they didn't understand what he was going through.

Tim spent two weeks at home lost in grief before deciding to return to work. But when he did, he noticed his coworkers kept making "the face . . . the one people make when they see you coming after your child has died." Over time, seeing that look got to be too painful, so Tim avoided people as much as he could and spent the next year walking around in a fog.

Coping with the death of a loved one is challenging under any circumstances, but particularly in the workplace. Although we often become close to our coworkers, we may not have the time, expertise, or emotional capacity to support a colleague in mourning. Most of us are uncomfortable around sadness. We struggle with what to say or how to help, often defaulting to saying nothing at all.

For those who've experienced a loss, work is an onerous place to be. There's often little to no privacy, especially for those who labor on a factory floor, stand in front of a classroom, or work in a cubicle in the middle of the room. At home, we can choose whom we interact with and, more importantly, whom we avoid. At work, we have no such agency. A coworker's thoughtless comment, no matter how well-intentioned, or the silence that so often greets a griever when they return to work can make an awkward situation untenable. Furthermore, each person's grief can look very different. One colleague might cry freely and openly and want to talk about the loved one who's died, while another might act as if nothing has happened, brushing off all attempts to bring up the loss. Even two employees grieving the same death may have divergent reactions, exhibit distinct behaviors, and approach the grieving process dissimilarly.

As a leader, your goal isn't to create a one-size-fits-all approach but to establish a basic framework of support and then adapt to the situation and person in front of you. To be truly effective in navigating grief in the workplace, you need to understand what grief looks like and learn how to tell when an employee needs more support than you and your team can provide.

Be aware of some of the more common myths about grief. For example, many people have heard that it comes in five stages. This is based on the model developed by Elisabeth Kübler-Ross, which was meant to describe the emotions a patient goes through when diagnosed with a terminal illness, not someone who is grieving a death. Another common misconception is that people "get over" their grief, but in fact, just as we never stop loving the person who died, we never stop grieving their absence. You'll likely have heard the aphorism "Time heals all things" applied to grief, as if the pain is guaranteed to ease over time in a linear fashion. The reality for many people is that the second year after a death is often harder than the first, and certain life events like weddings, funerals, graduations, and births will make grief more acute.

Above all, if you wish to be an effective leader, you will need to be creative and compassionate in meeting your grieving employees where they are. Be flexible as their need for help, support, and acknowledgment changes over time.

## The Emotional Impact of Grief

Grief is the natural response to loss of any kind. It's the pain you feel when someone or something you love dies or is taken away. Grievers often experience an array of emotions from shock or disbelief to guilt or regret to anger or profound sadness. Grief also has a physical impact, making it more difficult to sleep, eat, and think. The more significant the loss, the more intense the reaction, mentally, emotionally, and physically.

While each person expresses grief in different ways, most people will experience some combination of the following emotions:

- *Shock.* Right after the loss of a loved one, it can be hard to accept the reality of what happened, especially if the death was unexpected or out of order (for instance, the death of a child or younger sibling). People often feel numb and may have trouble believing their loved one is dead.
- *Sadness.* Profound sadness is the most universal symptom of grief. People often have feelings of despair, longing, loneliness, or emptiness after a death. They may cry frequently and uncontrollably.
- *Guilt.* After a death, people may feel guilty about things they said (or failed to say) or did (or failed to do). If the relationship was complicated or their loved one suffered for a long time, they may feel ashamed for feeling relieved. If their loved one died by suicide or overdose, they may feel guilty for not finding a way to prevent the death, even if they did everything they could.
- *Anger.* People may blame the doctors, other family members, God, themselves, even the loved one who died. They may be quick to become enraged over small issues, often

in a disproportionate way. They may feel out of sync with their coworkers, react oddly to innocuous comments, or be upset that life has gone on despite the death of their loved one.

- *Fear or anxiety.* A significant loss can trigger a range of worries. People often feel anxious, insecure, helpless, or afraid. They may worry about their own mortality or be scared about navigating life without their parent or partner, especially if they've been left with children to raise on their own.

## The Physical Impact of Grief

Although we tend to think of grief as an emotional reaction to loss, it manifests in physical problems as well, including but not limited to the following:

- insomnia
- exhaustion
- nausea and other digestive problems
- lack of appetite or significantly increased appetite, leading to weight loss or gain
- reduced immunity, leading to more frequent illness
- muscle or joint aches and pains
- lack of energy
- difficulty breathing
- tightness in the chest or throat
- heart palpitations
- headaches

# When Grief Is Prolonged

With time and compassionate support, most people's grief will ease as they find a way to move forward without their loved one. For a small percentage of people, however, their feelings of loss won't improve and will instead become a debilitating condition known as persistent complex bereavement disorder. In March 2022, the American Psychiatric Association changed the name to "prolonged grief disorder."

With prolonged grief, the emotions stemming from the death of a loved one can be so severe and long lasting that the griever will have trouble recovering from the loss and resuming their life. In the early stages, prolonged grief won't appear different from that of normal grief, but as time goes on, instead of the symptoms starting to fade, they'll continue or even worsen.

Doctors describe prolonged grief as being in an ongoing, heightened state of mourning that prevents healing, and they encourage grievers who still have intense feelings of grief or difficulty functioning a year or more after the death of a loved one to seek help from a mental health professional.

The signs of prolonged grief can include

- intense sadness about the death of a loved one that doesn't ease with time
- an inability to focus on little else but the loved one's death
- acute longing for the person who's died
- difficulty accepting the reality of the death
- loss of identity
- bitterness or rage about the loss
- feeling that life no longer has meaning or purpose
- difficulty reengaging with hobbies, activities, friends, or family

- suicidal thoughts
- alcohol or drug abuse
- emotional numbness
- heightened anxiety or fear
- intense loneliness
- an inability to enjoy life, even in small ways

Prolonged grief requires a clinical intervention, something beyond what you and your team can provide. Carefully assessing the situation and understanding your role as manager is critical. A newly single parent struggling to get to work on time may need more flexible hours. A grieving mother who fails to show up for work repeatedly without explanation more than a year after the death of her child may need help that you're not qualified to provide.

When Tim Moye returned to work at Delta Air Lines after the death of his son, he tried to repair what had happened to him on his own. As he recalled, "I was broken, and deep down inside, I knew I couldn't fix this. I tried to fix it. I tried to fix me. I really wanted to be able to do something that could make this all better."

A year later, a friend at work introduced Tim to a coworker named Kent Bishop, whose eighteen-year-old son had died in a car accident four months after Jason was found dead. The two men shared stories about their kids. They showed each other the tattoos they'd gotten in honor of their sons. They laughed; they cried; they hugged. Tim described it later: "Imagine a couple of old mechanics hugging each other in tears between Delta Air Lines' hangars. The mechanics who walked by us gave us plenty of space. It had been a year since Jason had died, and I had been stuck in a dark fog just going through the motions until that talk."

As Tim walked back to his office, he felt lighter having talked to someone who understood where he'd been and gone through what he'd experienced. This meeting between Tim and Kent was the catalyzing event for the creation in 2013 of Delta Air Lines' Wrenched Hearts, a peer support group for employees who have lost a child—at the time of this writing the only one of its kind in corporate America. (See Appendix 3 for more information.)

As a leader, you may not have the power to speed up the grieving process, but you do have the ability to listen and support your employees as they find their way forward. What's key is understanding how grief manifests, analyzing the behavior you're seeing, and then discussing the situation with your employee. You may discover there's more you can do than you realize or that a single, simple action will have a big impact. By showing compassion in all your interactions with the grieving employee, you can make space for them to work through their grief while continuing to be a valued, productive member of the team.

# 2

# The Business Costs of Grief

After my son died, both the CEO and the CFO spent time with me. The CFO had lost his little boy to an infection after a bone marrow transplant. He and I would spend one-on-one time in his office where we invariably wound up crying together about our sons. Did that increase my loyalty to the company? You bet.

—Trux Dolc

A FEW DAYS AFTER CATHERINE Lemmon Kearney returned to the California state agency where she works, she ran into the executive director in the hall.

"How are you doing?" the woman asked.

"I'm doing okay. Some days are better than others," replied Catherine.

"Really? Why?"

"Well, my husband just died . . ."

"Oh, of course, of course. I'm so sorry."

This uncomfortable exchange took place a few weeks after Catherine's husband, Bob, had passed away after a long illness. The agency's executive director had known Bob had died, but from the beginning she treated Catherine's return to the office as if everything was business as usual. Because Catherine had spent five months working remotely from Bob's hospital room, using up all of her vacation and sick leave, she could only take the agency's three days of bereavement leave.

When Catherine returned to work, she struggled to be as productive as she'd been in the past. Her mind wandered, and she frequently found herself just staring out the window. Her attention span shortened. She worked more slowly and could only do one thing at a time. She had flashbacks from the five months she spent in the hospital with Bob and from his last days at home. Those memories left her in tears and needing to end her day early and go home. She sat in meetings thinking, *Who cares?*, as the team discussed what now felt to her like trivial matters. Although she learned to adjust to the expectations of her workplace, her perspective never completely went back to normal.

Employees returning to work after the death of a loved one shouldn't be expected to function normally. Managers and coworkers often expect a grieving employee to recover rapidly from a life-altering loss and return to past levels of performance quickly. They assume the person must be doing better since they're back at work, not stopping to consider that they might now be the sole breadwinner and not have a choice about returning. Or that their need to be distracted from their grief is what allows them to be productive and focused when they are at work.

## How Grief Affects Productivity

Many organizations wrongly assume that grief's impact on productivity is confined to the person grieving, but no employee is an island. Errors, delays, and an inability to perform affect other people, projects, and departments. Organizations and leaders who dismiss or disregard their employees' grief pay dearly in the form of decreased productivity, tension within the team, diminished morale, higher turnover, and a damaged reputation.

A bereaved employee will often exhibit some combination of the following problems in their performance at work, all of which have a cost to the organization:

- trouble paying attention, concentrating, maintaining focus, or thinking clearly
- difficulty with recalling and retaining information
- lack of energy and motivation
- becoming easily offended or hurt by the words or actions of a coworker
- struggling with getting and staying organized
- diminished motivation
- difficulty making decisions and meeting deadlines
- inability to spot errors and mistakes

Bereaved employees will struggle with fatigue, cognition, and attention when they return to the workplace after the death of a loved one. They may have trouble showing up for work on time or at all. They often put on a brave front, not knowing how to ask for the assistance they need. Their body may be at their workstation, but their mind and heart are elsewhere.

## Why Grief Is Costly

In 2003 in what continues to be the only study of its kind, the Grief Recovery Institute (GRI) calculated that grief costs US businesses more than $75 billion a year due to absenteeism, diminished performance, and lost productivity, or $119 billion today. The GRI attributed 63 percent of the cost to the death of a loved one, close friend, or pet, with the remainder stemming from divorce, family crisis, financial catastrophe, and other causes. That number is certain to be higher during the COVID-19 pandemic. A 2020 study published in the National Academy of Sciences journal found that for every COVID-19 death, nine close family members are grieving. With over 1 million Americans dead of COVID in July 2022, there are at least 9.1 million people in mourning.

What makes grief in the workplace so expensive? An employee's diminished ability to concentrate is a significant factor. Of the 20,000 bereaved employees surveyed by the GRI, 50 percent reported at least thirty days in which a lack of concentration significantly affected their performance, and those numbers may well be higher than reported. Employees who struggle to concentrate can make costly mistakes or ill-advised decisions or fail to act when they should. They take longer to complete their work, leading to missed deadlines, lost sales, or unhappy customers. If the grieving employee is managing other people, the cost of their errors, late work, or inability to make decisions multiplies.

This struggle to concentrate can also be an accident waiting to happen. In its 2020 Workplace Safety Index, Liberty Mutual Insurance reported that of the ten leading causes of workplace injuries causing workers to miss work for more than five days, seven result from a reduced ability to remain focused and alert: vehicle crashes, several types of falls, collisions with an object, getting caught in equipment, mishandling objects (e.g., lifting a heavy box the wrong way). These injuries cost businesses more than $40 billion a year. In its survey, the GRI found that 50 percent of blue-collar workers reported a higher incidence of injury in the weeks following the death of a loved one.

Because American companies offer minimal time off for bereavement leave (the average is four days), most employees return to work in body alone. "Presenteeism" is the practice of coming to work despite illness, injury, or other conditions. The employee may be physically present in the workplace, but they may struggle to perform their duties and are more likely to make mistakes. According to a 2015 white paper produced by UL Workplace Health and Safety, presenteeism costs American companies more than $150 billion per year.

The GRI found absenteeism also increases after a death. Employees who received no support from managers or coworkers reported missing approximately thirty workdays each year, with 20 percent of employees continuing to miss workdays for more than a year.

## The Benefits of Supporting a Grieving Employee

Although every griever will struggle to be productive and present when returning to work, there are ways to help your employees continue to perform, mitigate their mistakes, and navigate those early painful weeks and months. Responding effectively and compassionately will not only help your grieving employee feel that their loss and pain are being acknowledged but enable them to perform better than they would have without support and to return to productivity more quickly. Other benefits include:

- reduced absenteeism
- less turnover

- fewer accidents and costly mistakes
- stronger, healthier workplace culture
- improved morale
- deeper loyalty to the organization

Fortunately for Catherine, her immediate supervisor was far more compassionate than the agency's executive director. Her boss reassured Catherine that she didn't need to work full days when she first returned and allowed Catherine to go home when she needed to, no questions asked. Catherine's boss "created a safe space when nowhere else felt safe." When Catherine expressed concern that she was only half as productive as before, her manager said, "Your half is better than most people's whole. Take as much time as you need."

She also regularly told Catherine how happy she was to have her back. She allowed Catherine to participate in a support group for grieving spouses at noon on Friday for ten weeks, telling Catherine to go home afterward. She took note of the date of Bob's death, and a year later, as the anniversary of his death approached, Catherine's manager offered her the day off. Years later, when Catherine forgot to ask for the day off on her wedding anniversary, her manager told her to take it, saying, "Come in late, leave early, don't come in at all. We've got you."

Catherine says that had her boss behaved like the executive director, she would have retired early, despite the huge financial hit. Instead, because her manager allowed her to trudge along at her own pace, she was able to compartmentalize her grief over time and return to productivity.

When two of her direct reports lost their spouses, Catherine knew her boss would support her decision to adjust their work-loads and allow them to attend the same ten-week bereavement group Catherine had gone to. She had not only the power to behave compassionately but also the confidence. Catherine said she would have felt awful if she couldn't have supported them in this way because she understood what they were going through and how badly they needed it.

## Grief and the Bottom Line

Death undermines everything we value about our work—control, personal growth, accomplishment, friendships with colleagues. When a leader isn't supportive, grieving employees become isolated at a time when they most need compassion and connection. Their grief can become disenfranchised if their loss isn't openly acknowledged and socially supported. When this happens, the grief becomes more intense, often prolonged. The bereaved employee disengages, leading to a deterioration in performance and productivity and a diminished commitment to the organization. This weakens the fabric of the team, potentially increasing the number of unhappy employees, and creates an unhealthy—if not toxic— work environment, exactly the kind of climate that causes employees to start leaving.

A 2022 study released by the *MIT Sloan Management Review* on what's been called the Great Resignation of 2021 found that a toxic corporate culture was 10.4 times more important than compensation in predicting turnover. Leaders and organizations that fail to support grieving employees are far more likely to experience bottom-line losses from declines in productivity, a decrease in employee engagement, a drop in employee retention, and a resulting increase in the cost of recruiting and hiring more people.

According to Gallup, replacing an exiting worker costs one half to two times the employee's annual salary. For an employee making a salary of $50,000, it will cost $25,000 to $100,000 to find a replacement and take five to eight months for them to reach full productivity.

In contrast, highly engaged teams are 14 to 18 percent more productive and 18 to 43 percent less likely to leave the organization. When employees know they can bring their grief to work, they don't have to expend extra energy trying to hide their sadness or ignore their pain. Although their productivity will be affected, especially in the short term, being able to work through their loss with the support of their boss and their team will help them return in time to prior levels of performance and deepen their attachment and loyalty to their colleagues and the organization itself.

# 3

# Supporting a Grieving Employee

As much as we want to reach out and help another person, the first way to help is to let them express what they're feeling. To just be there and not do anything. Then, once that hopefully cathartic process has happened, we can ask, 'What does support look like for you?

—Lisa Culp

TRUX DOLE SPENT THE FINAL three months of his son's life working from home. As the co-founder of HealthSparq, a soon-to-be-launched spinoff from Cambia Health Solutions, Trux had a sense of responsibility to the company, but working was also a way to stay sane. Gage had been three when he was diagnosed with Ewing's Sarcoma, five when he developed treatment-related leukemia, and seven when the Ewing's Sarcoma first recurred.

Trux had worked for three different companies since Gage's initial diagnosis as well as been on his own as a consultant. He'd also been unemployed for a period of time. Every transition brought its own form of stress, especially when it came to ensuring that the family had a health care plan that covered their son's cancer therapy.

After Gage's death at the age of nine, Trux went back to work in a haze. "I knew that partly for myself, but also for my wife, Lauren, we needed to take some time to reconnect. So many couples get divorced after a child dies. I got the idea to get out of the United States, away from where we are surrounded by our loss, after hearing that I was entitled to leave under the Family Medical Leave Act" (FMLA).

After talking with the company's human resources manager about the overhead and costs associated with FMLA, Trux was able to negotiate three months off by opting out of FMLA and using a manager's letter of approval securing his role and salary. He and Lauren bought round-the-world plane tickets and took Gage's ashes to all the places their son had wanted to go: Portugal, Italy, Egypt, China, Tibet, Thailand. Although the leave was unpaid, Trux's colleagues donated vacation days. One woman, who was notorious for never taking time off, donated all of the vacation time she'd accrued.

When Trux returned to work, he went straight into the volatile, demanding world of a startup. HealthSparq had received funding, and the team had six months to bring a product to market. Trux struggled with his grief. Although his team was compassionate, Trux felt his colleagues were sending a message that "we've said something about your loss. Now let's get back to work."

Trux had several challenging conversations with his manager and human resources and was eventually diagnosed with chronic, acute post-traumatic stress disorder (PTSD). "I had been in flight or fight mode for six years. Everything was triggering anger, hurt, and frustration over my ineffectiveness, my inability to make a difference or stop the inevitable. That began manifesting in my work interactions, so that when people on my team weren't delivering as expected, I went to anger."

Trux eventually sought help from a professional psychotherapist trained in the method called Eye Movement Desensitization and Reprocessing (EMDR), which has been shown to be effective in helping people recover from severe trauma. As Trux commented, "Having never been one for therapy or counseling, I was amazed at how helpful EMDR was. It dramatically improved my perspective, overall demeanor, and productivity."

During our waking hours, most of us spend more time at work than we do with our families. Coworkers can become dear friends, a chosen family. Become sick, break a leg, or have a new baby, and your work colleagues will usually show up for you. They'll ask how you're feeling or what they can do to help; they want to hear stories about the newest member of your family. But when a loved one dies, too many workplaces fail to do more than the bare minimum.

Close to 90 percent of all businesses in the United States offer at least a few days of bereavement leave, and many provide access to grief support. The boss might send flowers and a card, and a bereaved employee's colleagues may make meals or attend the memorial service. But once the employee returns to work, heavy with grief, the workplace often goes silent, not because people don't care but because they're afraid. Coworkers worry about reminding the grieving person about their loss, not realizing that they're thinking about their dead loved one all the time. Other employees don't want to ask how the griever is doing for fear of upsetting them, not understanding that silence is making the pain worse.

Managing and supporting a bereaved employee isn't easy, especially since each loss and every griever are different, but here are some actions you can take that will increase the chances your employee's return to work goes more smoothly and they get the support and compassion they need.

### Assess the situation.

What do you know about your employee's loss? What else do you need to know? Before you reach out, create a list of questions. Mark the ones you need answers to now, and only ask the others if your employee can handle the conversation. For example, consider the following:

1. What was your employee's relationship to the person who died? The death of a child, sibling, spouse, or parent is usually more shattering than that of a grandparent, distant relative, or pet. That said, if your employee was raised by her grandmother or lives alone with her dog, the grief may be just as intense.
2. How did the loved one die? An unexpected or violent death or a loss to suicide or drug overdose is more likely to add layers of guilt, remorse, shame, or regret to the sadness than would the death of an elderly relative after a long illness.
3. How recent is the loss?
4. Does the employee have a strong network of support outside of work? Someone without close family or friends will struggle far more than someone with a tight-knit family or group of friends.

### Make sure everyone knows what's happened.

Congratulating a new parent on the birth of a baby, only to learn the child was stillborn, is horrifying for both parties. Asking a colleague how her vacation went, only to find she was burying her brother, is mortifying. Don't assume that everyone in the organization has heard the news. Ask your employee what's appropriate to share, and provide some coaching to your team on what they might say when their grieving colleague comes back to work. Even if the bereaved employee doesn't want you to share much, you can still let their coworkers know that they've had a loss and will be away from work for a period of time.

When Käthe Nathan returned to work a few days after her mom died of metastatic breast cancer, one of the first coworkers she saw said, "How's your mom?" When Käthe told the woman that her mother had just died, her colleague said, "Whoa . . . so why are you here?" leaving Käthe feeling like a terrible daughter for coming back so quickly. Reflecting back on the incident twenty years later, Käthe believes her coworker would never have made such a hurtful comment if she hadn't been caught off guard by the news of her mom's death.

**Manage the re-entry.**

Set up a phone call with your bereaved employee before they return to work. Express your condolences, and ask how they're doing and what help you or your team can provide. Make it clear they shouldn't worry about work for now, that you and the team will take care of anything that arises, and they should focus on themselves and their family.

Offer the employee as much time off as you can. After Kelly Gallardo's husband died, her boss told her to take whatever time she needed. Kelly took six weeks off. When another colleague lost her husband, she took a month. Kelly said her company "has always been this way with our team members if there's a loss. Managers tell people to take whatever time they need because we know if people come back too soon, they'll just end up having a breakdown. There's no point in making someone who's suffered a significant loss come back to work so quickly."

Discuss the employee's plans to come back to work and what accommodations are needed and possible: working from home (if it's feasible), returning part-time initially, flexible hours, and so on. If they're nervous about seeing their coworkers for the first time, suggest that they come in for a few hours to see everyone and have those awkward initial conversations. They might also consider having their first day back toward the end of their work week in case the first few days are more painful than anticipated.

### Provide guidance to the team.

Ask the employee how they want to be treated when they return to work. Do they want to talk about their loss, or would they prefer to avoid the topic altogether? Do they want coworkers checking in to see how they're doing, or would they rather be left alone?

Chopi DeRose had been back at work for a few weeks after her husband, Dan, died by suicide when she sent an email to all of her colleagues. She recalled, "People wouldn't say Dan's name or talk about him. Instead, they just kept making sad faces at me. In my note, I gave them permission to bring Dan up. To say his name. To share stories and memories. To talk about him. I know they weren't intentionally trying to hurt me, but their silence was making everything so much worse."

### Acknowledge the grieving employee's loss, and encourage others to do the same.

Bring up your employee's loss in accordance with their wishes. Even though you've already acknowledged the loss and expressed your condolences, find a time when the two of you are alone to do it again. If they'd prefer not to discuss it at work, send a "no need to reply" text or email letting them know that you're thinking about them. Put a handwritten card on their desk or in their mail slot, or give them flowers or a gift card. Make it clear that you want to know how they're doing, and when and if they want to talk, you're willing and available.

Although everyone on the team knew that Marty Yee's sister had died, only a few of his coworkers acknowledged her death. "It's just so weird when something like this happens, and no one says anything to you. There were a few people who did, like my boss and a couple of close friends, and that stands out as a result," Marty recalled. "Everyone else was too nervous to say anything. It's a big event in your life, and the fact that no one talks about it is weird. It's not even that you need sympathy or comfort. It's just the elephant in the room, this huge thing that no one acknowledges."

### Designate a point person.

Ask the grieving employee whom they want to communicate with, in addition to you, once they return to work. The employee might prefer a close friend in another department, someone in a neighboring cubicle, or the human resources manager. Establishing a single point of contact means the griever won't have to communicate their needs, wants, and concerns to multiple people who may or may not share the information appropriately.

When a coworker is struggling, our instinct is to provide the kind of support we think we would want in a similar situation. When Käthe Nathan learned that one of her client's employees had lost her daughter in a car accident, she reached out to one of the woman's coworkers on the phone. "I said, 'I'm so sorry. When Nancy's back in the office, I'll be sure to reach out to her.' The other person said, 'Please don't. She doesn't want anyone to bring up her daughter's death.'" Käthe said it was so helpful to have that guidance. "Without it, I would have sent a card and made a point of mentioning her daughter's death the first time I talked to her. And that wasn't what she wanted."

## Be flexible.

It's difficult to concentrate when you're grieving. Your employee may need more time to finish a project. They may make more mistakes. They might struggle with certain aspects of their job or cry in meetings. Ask what they need taken off their plate and what they need extra help with. Consider offering a flexible schedule, the option to work from home (if feasible), or a reduction in hours until they're able to return full-time. Encourage them to take short breaks as needed or leave early when they're having a difficult day or want to attend a support group.

When Roger Harden returned to work after the death of his son TJ, he felt as though he was just going through the motions. "I was running the electrical discharge machines (EDM). I'm the expert at work. I can run the EDM blindfolded; I can troubleshoot it over the phone. It's second nature to me. So that's what I did. I took on all of the EDM projects, whether they were high on the priority list or not, and everyone was okay with that. I knew my brain wasn't there the way it should be, but I also knew that I had to be at work and keep my brain functioning. If nothing else, I had to keep moving."

## Allow for differences.

Some grieving employees return to work immediately because they have no choice as the primary breadwinner or provider of the family's health insurance, while others request extended leaves of absence. Some coworkers may want to talk about their loss all the time, while others may laugh and joke around with colleagues as if nothing has happened. You might think, "I'd never want so much time away," or "I wouldn't be able to tell jokes after something like that happened," but this isn't about you. It's about what's right for your employee.

Trish Kelly returned to the regional nonprofit where she works as a managing director two weeks after her husband died. "My work gave me purpose. It helped to normalize things for me and see a path forward."

Roger Harden also returned to work about two weeks after the death of his son. When his manager came in, he asked, "What are you doing here?" Roger said, "I can't sit at home." His manager nodded and said, "Fair enough."

The employee's needs and preferences can also change over time. Someone who initially doesn't want to talk about their loss may feel differently a few months later. Also, because it's difficult to know how it will feel being back at work, the employee may find they returned too quickly or that it's harder to be there than they expected.

Linda Knight Crane returned to her customer service job at Kohl's three weeks after her son Macauly died of an overdose. "I'd hear a song on the radio or think of Macauly, and start crying at my register. One of my colleagues would turn off the music, take over my line of customers, and urge me to take a few minutes by myself. My boss had told me to take as much time as I needed. I realized in these moments that I had come back too soon."

Marty Yee only took a few days off after the death of his sister but in hindsight wishes he had stayed away longer. He offered these suggestions to others who are grieving: "Take more time off than I did. Make space to confront your grief; take time to hang out with your family. I wanted to get back to work to keep my mind occupied instead of working through things. Spend time with your grief so that you have the space and time to process your loss."

**Address your workplace's unique challenges.**
After her thirty-two-year-old brother Chad died of a heart attack in July, history teacher Janell Sowers Cinquini had six weeks to prepare herself to return to the classroom. On the day Chad's obituary ran in the local paper, Janell stopped by the high school. When she walked into the main office and saw her boss, Janell began to

cry. The principal, Jenn Schiele, offered her condolences, telling Janell, "Whatever you need this year. We will give you whatever you need."

Once the school year started, Jenn checked on Janell frequently, making sure at a minimum that she made eye contact with her every day. "Teaching is such a strange position because you can be completely on your own," Janell explained. "You're not really alone, because you have thirty students in your classroom every hour, but you can go an entire day without seeing another adult. And that was an easy thing to do on hard days. Looking back, I can see that Jenn was keeping an eye on me without necessarily saying, 'How are you doing today about your brother?'"

Janell was also in the middle of a difficult pregnancy. After the obstetrician told her she couldn't stand for an entire class period, Jenn said, "Pick out a chair, and we'll buy it." The chair was in Janell's classroom the next morning.

Jenn told Janell that she would cover for her if Janell was having a hard day or class period. "That's the thing with teaching. I have to be on almost all of the time. Jenn was good at being there when times got tough or too emotional. I don't remember taking her up on her offer. I don't remember leaving my classroom for an extended period of time. But it was powerful knowing the option was there."

A K–12 teacher who is grieving will likely have to create a plan for the substitute in order to take time off. The sub plan can take several hours to create, which can be especially challenging in the face of a devastating loss. Years after Janell lost her brother, when another teacher had to take time off for a family emergency, Janell created his sub plans so that her colleague didn't have to.

**Treat your employee as you always have.**

If your employee was a capable, valued, trusted member of the team before their loss, continue treating them that way. Grief may have temporarily affected their performance, productivity, and work product; it hasn't turned them into a different person.

Christine Cosner's son was ill for eleven years before he died in 2019 at the age of twenty-nine. David was hospitalized frequently, went into a coma several times, and was placed on life support repeatedly. Christine's boss at PrintGlobe never questioned her need to be away from work, telling her, "Chris, you don't even need to tell me what's wrong. Just leave the office. If you're not there, we'll know what's going on."

Trux Dole believes that employers need to view a grieving employee like someone with a chronic ailment or hidden disability: "Grief is constantly cycling through a person's head. It's like having old anti-virus software running constantly on your computer. You can still get work done, but the computer will slow down, and you won't get the same level of efficiency. A grieving employee is trying to be productive, but their grief is constantly running in the background. As a leader, you'll want to show compassion and empathy, knowing your colleague is trying, all while acknowledging the constraints they're under, just as you would a chronic illness."

### Re-assess the situation.

How is your employee doing? Are you seeing any behaviors that have you concerned? Someone who cries at work a year or two after the death of a child may not be exhibiting signs of complicated grief but may be feeling the pain of secondary losses, like not getting to experience that child's graduation from high school or college or the opportunity to get married and have children.

Conversely, an employee who's withdrawn from their colleagues, frequently misses work without explanation, or can't seem to concentrate in meetings several years after the death of a distant relative may need the help of a mental health professional.

Could there be other factors causing the change in behavior? For example, is your employee now a single parent and sole provider for their family? Did they become their father's caregiver after the death of their mom? Has one of their children spiraled into depression, developed an addiction, or begun struggling academically? If so, the solution may not be mental health services, although those may help. Consider what you or the team can do to help your colleague during this difficult time, such as adjusting their workload or increasing the flexibility of their schedule.

As a manager, your role is not to become a therapist and diagnose your employee or provide counseling. Come across as merely sympathetic, and your colleague may think you're pitying him. Attempt to act as a counselor or therapist, and you will quickly find yourself in uncomfortable, even inappropriate territory. Instead, the goal should be to listen attentively, offer help and support, and watch for signs of distress or concerning behaviors. If you become worried about an employee's mental or physical health after a loss, encourage them to seek professional help, and do what you can to help them find it.

### Check in frequently.

In a few months, your employee might seem fine, even back to their old self. Keep asking how they're doing and what you can do to help. Acknowledge the anniversary of their loss, and offer them the day off if you can. Know that even if they've stopped mentioning their loved one at work, it doesn't mean they're no longer thinking about it. As Trish Kelly explained, "Just because a coworker looks okay doesn't mean he is. He may just have his work face on."

Every loss, circumstance, and grieving employee is different. Although it's helpful to have a basic framework of support in place—bereavement leave policies, access to grief resources and support—the key is to react to the individual employee in front of you. Acknowledge their loss, provide the accommodations they need (beyond what's in the employee handbook), create space for their grief at work, and continue supporting them as they find their footing, process their loss, and begin to heal.

4

# When an Employee Dies

People are looking to you to lead—to say,
'We can get through this. We've got the
systems and processes in place. We're here
to support you in whatever way you need.'

—Mark Ferdig

JIM CROSSEN SPENT EIGHTEEN YEARS at ESL Inc. in Sunnyvale, California, as a contracts manager before becoming the head of the American subsidiary of a multinational corporation. While he was still at ESL, the senior leadership team had to navigate the aftermath of a former employee killing seven coworkers and wounding four others. The CEO provided daily updates and held company-wide meetings to reinforce the message that "we are a family, and we are in this together." He and the other senior leaders acknowledged and honored the employees who died. Their actions created a road map for Jim to follow when he faced the heart attack, hospitalization, and death of a team member twenty-nine years later.

Less than two months after Jim became president and general manager of the subsidiary, the IT manager, Garth, had back-to-back heart attacks. Jim immediately reached out to Garth's ex-wife, staying in close contact during the month that Garth spent in the ICU. Jim also visited Garth several times. "Using the information I got from Garth's ex and from my visits, I kept my employees informed," Jim said. "I had to walk a fine line between respecting Garth's medical privacy and honoring their need to know what was happening, but I learned at ESL that this is just what you do. It's crucial, absolutely crucial, to communicate early and often, and to get the word out to everyone to the extent that's both legally permissible and okay with the family."

When Garth died a month later, Jim let his employees know. He organized a celebration of life and held a blood drive in Garth's honor as a thank you to the medical community who had taken such good care of him. "I kept my door open," Jim said, "and I do believe that people felt empowered and permitted to talk about personal stuff. The signals I sent were certainly consistent with that."

Although we may develop meaningful relationships with our coworkers, when one of them dies, we often aren't able to grieve the way we would for a close friend or family member. We may not be invited to the funeral. Our employer may not hold a memorial gathering for the person who's died. Because each employee knew the deceased in a different way, some colleagues may experience only a passing sadness, while others may be devastated. Some may want to talk about what's happened, while others may act as if nothing has changed. If senior leadership doesn't understand the importance of acknowledging the death, they may say nothing at all, leaving the team to deal with their grief alone.

Recognizing and honoring a dead employee is challenging. Yet to ignore or gloss over the loss of a coworker is to send a message to your remaining employees that their lives fail to matter to your organization once they're no longer part of it. More importantly, if you don't make space for employees to express their grief and pay tribute to their deceased coworker, their emotions and resentment can spill out in ways that will cost your company in lost productivity, damaged morale, or the departure of valued employees. Here are the steps to take that will enable you to navigate the aftermath of an employee's death.

### Contact the deceased employee's family.

Make the phone call at a location and time when you're unlikely to be interrupted and when you're prepared to sit with your sadness and that of the family member. Begin by expressing your condolences; then ask what the family would like shared about the death. Inquire about whether there will be a memorial service and whether you and your team may attend. Find out whether the family would prefer a donation instead of flowers and whether they have any immediate needs like meals, groceries, or financial support for medical or funeral expenses. Before you end the call, determine who in the family is their preferred point of contact and the best way to communicate with that person.

It's important to reach out as soon as you can after the death, as the funeral may happen quickly, depending on the employee's culture and religion. In the Jewish tradition, for example, funerals usually take place one day after the death, although there is allowance for delaying the burial to allow family and friends to attend. The first seven days after the funeral are known as shiva, a time when the immediate family remains at home and receives guests who have come to pay their respects and support the bereaved.

In the Muslim tradition, Islamic custom dictates that the body be buried before sunset on the day of the death or at least within twenty-four hours. Mourning for a close relative lasts for three days, although there's a special mourning period for women who have lost a husband, lasting for four months and ten days. During that time, a Muslim woman doesn't wear perfume or jewelry, and she only leaves the house to run errands or go to work. During the three days of mourning after the funeral, it's traditional to reach out to the family and bring them food so they don't have to worry about cooking.

Christian funeral services usually take place about a week after the death. Wakes and viewings are usually held a few days ahead of the funeral, but sometimes on the same day. Both offer mourners an opportunity to share their condolences. A viewing, or visitation, is more informal, whereas a wake is a traditional Catholic ceremony. After the funeral, mourners usually gather at the church or at the home of a family member.

### Gather the team.

Meet with employees in person if possible, starting with the deceased employee's immediate coworkers, and then with the rest of the organization as soon after the death as possible. Convey whatever details are appropriate to share as well as what you'll be doing on behalf of the company to honor the loss initially—such as a card, flowers, or a charitable donation. Allow ample time and space for people to react, ask questions, and share their sadness. Encourage everyone who knew the employee to send a note to the family sharing a story or memory and what they'll miss or what they valued about their colleague. Call the employees who couldn't attend to be sure they hear the news from you and not secondhand.

Because of his experience at ESL, Jim Crossen understood when he gathered his employees to tell them about the death of the company's IT manager that "the key for a leader is to be present, genuine, and in the moment, even though you have general manager sh*t running around your brain. It's absolutely crucial to be in the moment when you're tending to these actions."

When one of the employees at Society for the Blind died, Shari Roeseler, the executive director, called the staff together to share the sad news. "I told them that anyone who wanted to go home should go home. I paid for Ubers so no one had to take public transportation. I gave the deceased employee's department the entire week off, and I offered everyone grief counseling."

Remember to be sensitive to your employees' ability to handle the news. After telling her team the news about their colleague's death in person, Debbie Maus allowed anyone who wanted to work from home that day to leave, saying, "We will all process this news differently." A few hours later, she gathered everyone on Zoom and told them, "I just want us to be together. You don't have to say anything if you don't want to, or you can share a memory of Kelly. I have a few that I'm going to share." After Debbie finished speaking, she left the space open. A few colleagues shared stories. After about thirty minutes, Debbie ended the call.

### Inform everyone else.

As appropriate, contact the board of directors, clients, customers, donors, vendors, volunteers, the general public, and the media, beginning with those most affected by the death. Share whatever information you can, let them know who will be taking over the deceased employee's responsibilities in the short term and encourage them to contact you directly with any questions or concerns. Be prepared for more probing questions if the death happened at work or is seen as newsworthy, but try to focus the conversation on how much the employee meant to your organization and how you plan to honor them and navigate the loss.

### Cover your deceased employee's responsibilities.

Change their voicemail and set up an auto reply to their email. Redirect both to the person responsible for responding to the messages. Determine who has access to the employee's desktop computer, laptop, office, files, company cell phone, and any other equipment or systems and how you'll get access if you don't currently have it. Meet with the team members who will be covering the deceased employee's responsibilities to determine what needs to get done and divide up the work. Set up regular check-in meetings to be sure nothing falls through the cracks and no one is feeling overburdened or resentful about the extra work.

If the death happened at work, provide appropriate support to those most affected by it. After branch supervisor Amber Clark was murdered at six p.m. in the North Natomas Library parking lot, Sacramento Public Library's two deputy directors took turns working at the branch every day. One deputy director went to the branch at closing time every night for weeks because, as he said, "I'm just going to make sure everyone's okay when they leave the building."

### Ask HR to contact the family.

The human resources team can make arrangements to issue the final paycheck and inform the family about any life insurance, retirement fund distributions, workers' compensation benefits, accidental death coverage, COBRA health insurance, and so on available to the survivors.

### Create space for people to talk about the loss and share their sadness.

Let your employees know that they are welcome to share stories and memories about their colleague at the next team or all-staff meeting. Consider asking one or two people to speak first so others feel more comfortable sharing. Begin the meeting by offering your thoughts about the deceased employee and asking for a moment of silence. Call on those who've agreed to go first; then open the floor for anyone else who wants to speak. Allow employees to gather informally as needed to mourn and process their grief. Keep a watchful eye on those who were closest to the deceased in case they need extra support.

### Arrange for grief support.

The death of a colleague can trigger a host of unexpected reactions that may require professional help to process: sadness about the loss of a friend, fear about one's own mortality, guilt over an argument or unpleasant final interaction with the deceased, regret over a damaged professional relationship that can no longer be repaired. A trained mental health professional can help your team, both individually and collectively, understand their feelings and can offer ideas on how to address them. This is particularly important if the employee died on the job, in a violent manner, or by overdose or suicide.

Sacramento Public Library director and CEO Rivkah Sass used some of the insurance settlement after the branch supervisor's murder to pay for counseling for a year for any employee who wanted it. She gave the staff who had worked with the deceased employee and all of the staff who were in the building when she was killed a week off, telling them, "If you need more time, just let us know, and we'll give you administrative leave." Rivkah and the library's leadership team wanted employees to understand that they cared enough to help them get through this. "I don't care if they use their time off to get a pedicure. That's not our business. We want them to know we care about them, that we care enough to help them get through this."

**Celebrate your colleague.**

Hold a memorial service or gathering to honor your deceased employee. Invite the family, and ask if they would like to speak. Include others outside the organization (e.g., board members, clients, volunteers, donors) who knew the employee well. Choose a few people to speak about what your colleague meant to them and the organization. Serve their favorite dish or dessert. Create a photo memory board or video. Set up a table with blank note cards and pens, ask people to jot down a story or memory, and give the cards to the family.

After the death of his IT manager, Jim Crossen tracked down the man's sister and invited her to a company memorial service. He invited the manager's ex-wife and son, all of the current employees, and any former employees who wanted to attend. At the gathering, Jim paid tribute to the manager and invited anyone else who felt comfortable to speak. Then Jim organized a company-wide blood drive in his honor. As he explained, "My goal was to convey by my behavior and my actions that we are a family, and we have lost one of our own."

**Contact the family about their loved one's belongings.**

Offer the family choices about how to manage the employee's personal property at work. Does the family want you or a team member to pack everything up, or would they prefer to do it? Do they want to pick up the boxes or should you drop them off? Inquire about any company property your employee had at home—keys, laptop, cell phone, files—and make arrangements to retrieve it.

**Be sensitive to your employees' reactions.**

You may not be able to wait for long to hire a replacement or reassign the deceased employee's workspace. What's most important is that there are no surprises about the timing of the packing up or the need to put someone else in their spot and no confusion as to the reason why. Be open about the timeline and process as well as your plans for hiring a replacement.

Because the Crocker Art Museum was short on custodians and already planning to hire more, Michelle Maghari, the director of Visitor and Building Services, didn't have to announce she was replacing an employee who had died, but could instead say that her department was adding more custodians to their staff. "I wanted to handle hiring in a way that was thoughtful and compassionate," she said.

### Decide how to honor your colleague.

Here are some ideas:

- Create a video or memory book with photos and stories.
- Contribute annually to a cause or nonprofit that was important to your deceased employee.
- Establish a scholarship or award in the employee's honor.
- Name a conference room, break room, or other area of the workplace after your employee.
- Install a workplace memorial: plant a tree or garden; install a commemorative bench; hang a plaque or piece of art.
- Hold a yearly fundraiser, or volunteer as a team for a day of service.

Using funds from the insurance settlement, the Sacramento Public Library was able to remodel the teen space at the library where branch supervisor Amber Clark was murdered. Rivkah explained, "We got new furniture. We painted. We bought really cool equipment, and we renamed it the Amber Fawn Wooton-Clark Teen Space. Amber was in charge of the accessibility team, so every

May, in honor of her birthday, the library holds a film festival, arranges for speakers like Temple Grandin, and offers programs about accessibility."

### Address employees' concerns.

If the deceased was an executive or senior leader, employees may be nervous about what will happen with their team or department. If the deceased was the CEO or owner of the company, they may worry about whether they'll have a job. Provide what information you can, and be honest when you don't know or can't yet share. Encourage the team to come to you if they have questions or concerns or need extra support or access to grief counseling or other resources.

Michelle Maghari didn't want to put her team members, who are private people, "in an uncomfortable position by asking them to share their grief. Instead, I gave them space to tell me what would help them feel better and continue moving forward. I watch and listen to what they need. I ask how they're doing and what I can do to be supportive of them."

### Continue to remember your deceased colleague.

Send a card to their surviving partner or child on the anniversary of their death. Continue saying their name at work, and encourage your colleagues to share memories and stories of your time together. Gather once a year in their memory for a meal or charitable activity.

After one of her program directors died, Debbie Maus and her team set up an educational fund for the woman's two-year-old son and included it in the memorial notice they sent out so that their nonprofit association members could donate. Debbie invited the deceased director's husband to the holiday luncheon and acknowledged what would have been her four-year work anniversary a few months later.

Three days after branch supervisor Amber Clark was killed in the parking lot, Rivkah Sass organized a memorial service on the third floor of the main library. Not until she was well into the planning did Rivkah remember that two librarians had been killed in that same location twenty-five years earlier. After the gathering, two employees who had worked for the library when the first shooting happened approached Rivkah to thank her, saying, "We were never given this opportunity [after the first incident]. I feel like I'm grieving all over again for my lost colleagues." Their comments were a gut punch—a reminder of the way we don't acknowledge grief and death in the workplace—but they also validated what Rivkah had done. As she explains, "You do the best you can. You can't plan something to be perfect. You can't plan for the right thing. You offer it up. I'm so grateful I said, 'We have to do this. We have to bring everyone together. We have to let the staff know that this is terrible but we are in it together.'"

# 5

# Grieving When You're the Boss

I became a better leader because of the experience of losing my mother. More empathetic. Better at prioritization and living in the present. My mother's death reminded me of the smallness of what our company does and its importance at the same time.

—Andrea Corradini

IN LATE 2014, THIRTY YEARS after Anne Hed and her husband, Steve, launched Hed Cycling together, the company's future looked bright. Hed had just introduced Big Fat Deal, the first carbon fat-tire rim for snow bikes; Cervélo Cycles, a manufacturer of racing and track bicycles, had asked Steve to design a one-piece molded carbon bike frame; and the company was moving into a new space in December that would double the size of their existing operation.

The day the engineers from Cervélo came to see Steve's prototype frame, Anne left the meeting early to pick up their daughter from school. Steve called as she headed home to say, "Annie, we made it. It's beautiful, and it works, and they want us to make their frame." This was the last conversation they ever had. Later that afternoon, Steve collapsed in the parking lot on his way to dinner with the Cervélo engineers. He never regained consciousness and died four days later.

For any leader who's suffered a devastating loss, finding a way to navigate the aftermath while continuing to run the organization is a significant challenge. Because no two leaders grieve the same way, some may need weeks or months away from work to process their loss and regain their footing, while others may discover that being at work is what lets them keep the loss at bay until they're ready to face their grief. Regardless of the path you take, offering your team guidance on how to work with and support you during this difficult time will help avoid painful, uncomfortable situations and enable you to better handle both your grief and your professional responsibilities.

**Tell the team what's happened.**

Whether you ask someone else or do it yourself, let your employees know you have lost someone dear to you, disclosing only as much about the circumstances as you are comfortable sharing. As awkward as it is to acknowledge a death, it's far worse to have someone ask where you went on vacation and have to explain that you were burying your son. Interactions like that will be excruciating for you and embarrassing for your employees, who may also worry about how this unintentional gaffe will affect your opinion of them.

**Return to work when you feel ready.**
Unless you absolutely have to return immediately, don't rush back to work. It's better to take a few extra days or weeks than to come back prematurely and find you're not able to function. The work will get done. Members of your team will step up. The organization will survive your absence. Your employees and customers will understand your need to be away.

Linda Knight Crane returned to her job at Six Flags Great Adventure three weeks after her son Macauly died of an overdose, only to realize she had come back too soon. She later reflected, "You should take off as long as you want. It helps. Only you know what needs to be done, whether and when you can go back to work. And if you find you've gone back too soon, then you should leave."

On the other hand, there's nothing wrong with going back to work after a week or even a few days if what you need is a return to normalcy.

Although Society for the Blind's board chair told executive director Shari Roeseler to take as much time away from work as she needed after her brother died, Shari chose to return to the office a week later. "For me, there was a need to get some routine back, something that felt like normal life at a time when it felt like the world had shifted on its axis. It was my choice to come back."

**Prepare for colleagues and employees asking how you are.**
While many colleagues will say nothing about your loss, some will ask how you're doing without knowing how to react to your answer. To avoid situations where you have to comfort or reassure them, prepare a response in advance.

When Jody and Robert Nelsen returned to work at the University of Texas at Dallas after their only child, Seth, died by suicide, they came up with an answer in response to inquiries about how they were doing. "We told people, 'We're coping,'" Jody said. "You don't want to say, 'I'm fine.' And you don't want to say, 'Horrible! What do you think?' Telling people that we were coping took care of the conversation. People would say, 'Oh good. I'm so sorry.' And we'd go on with business."

### Brace yourself for people's (often unintentionally) hurtful comments.

Your colleagues will struggle with what to say to you. They may compare your loss to one of their own, either human or animal; they may minimize what's happened, thinking that they're being comforting; they may offer a platitude or share a belief about where your loved one is now.

For one manager, who was shattered by the death of both of her parents in a three-year period, it was coworkers telling her that "time heals everything" over and over again. "Time isn't healing it," she explained. "You're teaching yourself to live with not being able to talk to your dad or call your mom as well as the pain of not getting those calls. You are still going to miss your parents. I think about mine every day." For another, it was a colleague saying, "Oh, you have a lot of life left to live. You're going to meet someone," after the death of her husband. Although comments like these may add to your pain, remember that your employees may not know how to react, and they usually mean well.

Even innocuous questions can be painful. After Seth died, Jody and Robert made a plan on how to respond to the question, "How many children do you have?" Because they didn't want to deny their son's existence, they would say, "We had a son, but we lost him a year ago." Once Robert became president of the University of Texas–Pan American, they'd say, "We lost our son to suicide, but now we have thirty thousand kids." They felt that putting a lighter spin on it made the situation less awkward and uncomfortable.

### Ask for what you need.

Andrea Corradini, global vice president of the Kids Footwear Division at Nike, spent eight months flying back and forth between Oregon and Utah to care for her mother, who was dying of lung cancer. A few days after the funeral, Andrea's team was flying to Japan for a marketing trip. Andrea called her boss and asked to go, saying, "I need to go on this trip. I have to get out of here and be in a completely different environment. Is that okay? I could be a train wreck." Her boss's response was "Get on the plane."

For Andrea, the trip to Japan "was amazing because I got to leap into an unfamiliar world that had no signals or symbols or anything that reminded me of Salt Lake City, where my mother had lived and died. I cried a lot, but I also smiled a lot. I started to process my loss there."

### Educate your employees about grief and loss.

Not everyone who works for you will have experienced the death of someone close to them. Thus, what you say, how you act, and the choices you make may be confusing to other people. It may not be what they envision doing in a similar situation. You don't owe them a rationale or even an explanation, but to avoid having to deal with their critical reactions or judgment, it will help to create a context and understanding of why grieving people make some of the decisions they do in the workplace when dealing with a significant loss. Suggest some resources (see Appendix 1), arrange for training, hire a consultant, or ask one of the members of your leadership team to facilitate a conversation about grief and loss and the choices leaders make when they return to work.

### Establish boundaries.

If you work in a culture that normally expects you to respond 24/7, let your team know when you'll be available, when you won't, and how you want to be contacted after hours. Reserve time on your calendar to work undisturbed in your office, and be sure to take time away from work on the weekends.

### Offer your team guidance.

When, where, and how should your colleagues express their condolences? Do you want them to bring up your loss at work? Ask how you're doing? Or would you prefer to focus exclusively on work and work-related topics? If they see you looking upset, should they check on you or leave you alone?

When one manager's father died, she didn't know how to deal with her grief and preferred not to think about it at work. "People will bring up your loss with good intentions. If it's too painful to discuss, it's okay to say, 'I don't want to talk about it.' Then say what you want instead. Everyone will respect that. My colleagues got the message, but you have to let them know."

The woman who worked just outside Linda Knight Crane's office stopped her one day and said, "I can hear you crying in your office. Should I get up and hug you? Or should I ignore you?" Linda told her to ignore it because "I'm going to be doing it all day."

Andrea Corradini found it helped to be direct: "The hardest part about grief is that you just don't know when it's coming. I'd have a full day of meetings, and I couldn't get out for my run because there was too much going on, so I had no release valve. I'd be sitting in a conference room, and this tear would appear. People would freeze. I'd say, 'I'm good. This just has to come out right now.'"

She recalled, "I told people that as hard as it was to watch my seventy-two-year-old mom die, it is the order of the universe. And it was hard. It was the hardest thing I've ever done. But it was not my child. That's not circle of life. That's not fair. I used to say this to make people feel comfortable, to help them understand that I was okay. And yes, I'd love a hug." By calibrating her grief for her team, Andrea gave them permission to approach her about it.

### Allow yourself to be less productive.

When you're grappling with grief, it takes more time, energy, and effort to finish a project or complete a task. Divide deliverables into small chunks. Work in short bursts; then take a break to clear your head. Allow extra time to meet your deadlines. Assess your workload, determine what you will and won't be able to do, and then focus on what's most important. Create a "stop doing" list, and share it with a few colleagues to be sure you assign those tasks to others.

### Write everything down.

Grief can cause confusion and forgetfulness and make it challenging to concentrate. While both normal and expected after a significant loss, this "brain fog" may have you struggling to keep track of your appointments and assignments. Capture what you need to accomplish on a list or in your calendar, rather than trying to remember meeting times and deadlines the way you might have in the past. Print out emails you need to respond to. Invite your team to remind you about commitments you've made and projects you haven't finished.

Trux Dole offers this advice: "Compartmentalize your work and make lists. Break down projects and assignments into small, bite-size pieces. The smaller, the better. Use the notes app on your phone, use a pad, use a planner. Write everything down, and don't let the lists overwhelm you."

### Set up support outside of work.

You'll need ways to process your grief, and talking to the people who work for you is rarely an appropriate choice. Find a grief group. See a therapist. Talk to friends and family. Your sadness may make your employees uncomfortable, and without a safe, suitable outlet, you may find it spilling over at work.

When one of her employees died after a long battle with cancer, Debbie Maus was grateful for her therapist's help as she processed the loss. "You need someone walking alongside you who has professional work experience in grief counseling and is only seeing the situation through your eyes. You need someone who can help you process and, when there's nothing to say, someone who will sit with you in silence."

## Pick a point person.

Choose someone you trust who will give you honest, direct feedback about the ways your team is struggling to communicate with you or what's making them uncomfortable. It should be someone who feels comfortable pointing out the ways your grief may be coloring your analysis of a situation or another employee, who will direct a nosy coworker to stop asking questions, deal with a colleague's hurt feelings if grief has you acting cranky or distracted, and coach your employees on the best way to share a concern or interact with you.

## Let your team know how to work with you.

Tell your colleagues and employees the best way to communicate with you, both in the workplace and at home (e.g., text, email, Slack, phone call), and how quickly they should contact you again if you don't respond. Caution them that you may be quicker to get frustrated or irritated, and they shouldn't take it personally. Forewarn them that you may take more days off or leave work early on hard days.

When Shari Roeseler returned to work after the death of her brother, she met with her leadership team, telling them, "I may very well forget things that I said I would do or things that you tell me. Even though I feel like I'm here, I know that I'm not. I know enough about the grieving process to know that it can leave you with cotton upstairs. Please be patient with me. I also know that my own patience with other people, especially with people who whine or complain, is on a short fuse right now."

**Do what you need to do, but make space for your grief.**
You don't have to pretend to be okay. And it's okay if you want to pretend. Just know that eventually, you will have to face your grief.

Anne Hed, like many leaders, went into "powering through" mode after her husband, Steve, died. She explained, "What I ended up doing was going into survival mode, which meant going full gas forward. Making sure I was mother hen. Making sure my kids were okay. Pouring all this energy into the business, my employees, my family. As a result, my employees powered through with me. Their attitude was 'Let's go for it!'"

When Anne looks back, she wishes she'd known to offer some type of counseling to her employees. "They saw me powering through and being so strong that I missed some of the signs that people were really hurting. I only saw this two, three, four years later. I know some of them were grieving, and I didn't see it."

**Prioritize your health.**
Sleep. Hydrate. Eat well. Go for a run or long walk. Shut your office door and meditate or sit quietly for a few moments. Call a close friend. Leave early or come in late on the hard days, especially if you're feeling exhausted. Your team will be watching. They'll want to know you're taking care of yourself, especially if you don't want to discuss your grief or share how you're doing at work.

**Reach out to other leaders for advice and perspective.**
Navigating your own grief can be both exhausting and all-consuming. It's easy to get stuck or struggle to figure out what to do on your own. Find a peer group or trusted colleague outside of the organization in whom you can confide. After Rand Construction president Jon Couch died in a plane crash, CEO Linda Rabbitt turned to Robb Johnson at Jones Lang LaSalle Inc. for advice. He created a two-page memo that was designed to help Linda think through a ninety-day plan and what she needed to do. She explained, "He

said protect your people by giving them calm reassurance that the company is safe, the clients are in good hands, and the future is strong. Be active and visible inside and outside Rand as a calming, focused, deliberate, compassionate, and confident leader. Set up weekly meetings with key internal Rand people regarding issues you need to face. Avoid big decisions. Be gentle and nice to yourself. Get some sleep; don't do too much."

### Reassure your team.

Your employees will worry about the viability of the organization, the security of their jobs, and what will happen if you aren't able to handle your grief. Even if you are struggling, reassure them that their jobs are safe, you will be okay in time, and the organization will continue to thrive.

After Steve's funeral, Anne Hed returned to work, telling her employees that they would be moving as planned into the new, larger space that Steve had helped design. She said, "I wanted them to understand that we were moving forward. It turned out to be a blessing not to have to go back to the building where Steve had died day after day after day." Anne also began calling herself the CEO because she realized her employees were worried about the future of Hed Cycling now that their charismatic leader was dead.

### Prompt yourself to pause.

Take a breath before responding to an unhappy employee. Go for a walk before returning a call from an angry customer. Draft the email, but wait until morning to send it. Run your planned written or verbal response by a trusted colleague to be sure you're not over-reacting or misinterpreting what someone said or did.

Shari Roeseler at Society for the Blind said she would hear herself sounding more curt than she intended. "I'd have an email response to send and think, 'No, I can sit on this one. It won't be as gracious as it should be if I send it now.'"

When you're grieving, you're also more likely to make mistakes. Check your figures one more time, or ask a colleague to do it for you. Put the document aside, and read it over in the morning when you're fresh. No matter your role or responsibilities, it's important to breathe and take your time when your brain is preoccupied by grief. Roger Harden said, "For me, for most machinists, we hate making mistakes. We hate getting things wrong. We hate missing details, and we hate scrapping a part. But if you can take a pause, take measured steps, do what you know how to do, but do it in the way you know how to do it, you can still get the job done, and your odds are better of getting it done correctly."

### Give yourself grace.

Weighed down with grief, you may find yourself snapping at an employee or bursting into tears at a team meeting. You may feel stressed, anxious, or emotional. You are, as Anne Hed points out, carrying your grief, the grief of your children or other family members, and the grief and anxiety of your employees. Remind yourself that you are doing the best you can navigating a painful, challenging time. Remember, too, that your grieving process is your own.

As history teacher Janell Sowers Cinquini learned after the death of her brother, "You're going to have bad days, weeks, months down the line. You're going to have a bad day on your loved one's birthday or on another significant date, maybe ten years down the road. I think I cry harder now, realizing how long it's been. Chad should have been here to turn forty."

"Be patient with yourself and go gently," Shari Roeseler counseled. "Don't compare how you grieve to how somebody else does. We all grieve in our own way, and there's no one right way to do it. In time, the wallop of grief will simmer down and not feel so heavy."

# 6

# Grief Support in a Virtual Workplace

People are going to say the wrong thing because they don't know what to say. Arm your employees with three things to say and not to say. Keep it simple.

The best:

1. Just know that I am thinking about you.
2. I appreciate you and the way you are working through your grief.
3. Hang in there; this is going to be a long road.

The worst:

1. You will get through this.
2. I can't imagine how you must be feeling.
3. How are you feeling?

—Trux Dole

Dᴜʀɪɴɢ ᴛʜᴇ ᴘᴀɴᴅᴇᴍɪᴄ, ʟᴏss ɪs everywhere, yet the support a grieving employee desperately needs can be even harder to come by when the team is working online or in a hybrid work environment. In those settings, we lose the small, serendipitous moments of comfort that come from running into a colleague in the hallway or by the coffeemaker. An impromptu opportunity to check in or offer to go for a walk. A reassuring hand on the shoulder or quick word of support as everyone takes their seats before a meeting.

After her in-person team transitioned to remote work during COVID, Danilyn Rutherford, president of Wenner-Gren Foundation, discovered that "on Zoom, you really have to pay attention to pick up when something is going on for your colleagues." An employee's sadness can go unnoticed, as can their struggle to concentrate on work, when the only interaction with coworkers is virtual. It's hard to see red eyes or read facial expressions on a screen. During team meetings, you may jump right into the agenda without remembering to check in with everyone, and even when you do, your employee may not feel comfortable answering honestly.

Grief support is difficult to navigate when we are working in the office; in a remote environment, it takes even more effort and thought. How can you ensure a grieving employee is getting the help and support they need when the team isn't together in the office every day?

**Contact your employee as soon as you hear the news.**
Express your condolences using more than one form of communication—voice mail, text, Slack, email—to be sure your employee gets the message. Ask to talk on the phone so that you can understand what support they need immediately, what's appropriate to share about their loss, and how you can help. Since the team is working remotely, determine whether there's anything you need to pick up to cover the employee's projects and assignments while they're on leave.

Whenever an employee at the Society for the Blind suffers a loss, executive director Shari Roeseler always checks in as to what she should and shouldn't tell the other members of the team. "I want to know exactly what I can and can't share, and I want my colleague to tell me how they want the story told."

### Share the news.

Let the other employees know what's happened, how you and the organization will be acknowledging the loss, and the best way for the team to do the same. If appropriate, provide details about the memorial or funeral service, and invite them to attend. Encourage them to send notes of condolence and support to their grieving team member. Distribute your employee's projects and assignments, and instruct everyone to contact you, not the griever, if they need direction or more information.

### Create a re-entry road map.

When your grieving employee is ready to return to work, set up a phone or Zoom call to discuss whether they'll need accommodations (such as a temporary reduction in hours, a later start time so they can drop the kids off at school, or a few hours off each week to attend a grief support group). Review the employee's commitments, responsibilities, and deadlines, and discuss what they think they can and can't do. For example, if talking on the phone feels too difficult, ask them to focus on proposal writing or data analysis instead. Encourage them to tell you if anything feels difficult or overwhelming so you can make timely adjustments.

### Ask for guidance for the team.

Does your grieving employee want their colleagues to bring up the loss on phone calls or during Zoom meetings? Should coworkers call to ask how the employee is doing or how they can help? Or would the griever prefer to be the one to bring it up?

## Educate your employees about grief.

Make sure your team has a basic understanding of how to support someone who's experienced a significant loss. Caution them against making some of the more common mistakes such as comparing, ranking, or diminishing losses based on who died or how they died; telling the bereaved employee they know how they feel; or offering religious platitudes such as "Your son is in a better place" or "God needed another angel."

Provide some simple examples of what to say and do, and remind them they have no power to fix the situation or make anything better. Explain that what their colleague needs most is an acknowledgment of what's happened, a sympathetic ear if they want to talk, and specific offers of help to lighten their load.

## Set expectations, and adjust as needed.

Coach your employees that their coworker may show up differently from how they did before their loss. The griever may work odd hours, be less responsive, or take longer to get their work done. They may make choices others don't understand or agree with, like coming back to work a few days after their spouse dies. The griever may prefer to interact by Slack or text instead of Zoom or phone. Encourage them to avoid judging and instead offer their coworker grace and understanding. They don't need to approve of everything the griever is doing, but they do need to support their colleague.

Linda Jellison's employers were kind and supportive after her mother died, telling her to take whatever time off she needed. As Linda reflected back on those early days of loss, she offered advice to other employers looking to be supportive of a grieving employee: "She may need time off. She may have trouble finishing projects. She may have trouble focusing. Don't expect her to work the same long hours right after she returns to work. Allow her to take time off if she needs it."

**When an opportunity to connect appears, lean in.**
During the first year of the pandemic, high school history teacher Janell Sowers Cinquini had a student whose father had died when she was in eighth grade. One day on Zoom, Janell asked the student about an item visible behind the student, which turned out to have something to do with her father. Janell recalled, "After that, there were multiple days when the student would log off last in order to tell me something about her dad. I could tell it was hard, but she also wanted to talk about him."

**Create a check-in plan.**
Set up a weekly phone or Zoom meeting with your grieving employee. Ask questions like "How did last week go?" "What are you finding difficult?" "Is your workload manageable?" "What do we need to adjust or change?" "Where do you need extra help or support?" "How can I help you in the coming week?" If it's safe and possible to do so, get together in person periodically, as your colleague may feel more comfortable opening up when you're face-to-face. In between the scheduled calls, check in frequently during the early months to be sure there aren't any urgent issues that the employee is struggling with alone at home.

**Encourage the employee to take advantage
of working from home.**
Tell them it's okay to have their camera off in meetings whenever they need to. That they can take a break or short walk to compose themselves before they return a client call. After her mother died, Linda Jellison found that there were benefits to working remotely. "When you get sad, you can let the voicemail pick up. You have a quiet, private space to be alone or have a good cry. You can step outside for a few moments or make yourself a fresh cup of coffee." It's also much easier to put on your "work face" when you don't want to talk about your loss.

**Focus on what needs to get done, not how it gets done.**
Your employee may have trouble sleeping and prefer to work late at night. They may start working early in the morning, work in short bursts, or take more time off. They may need time during the workday to sit and grieve. As long as the assignments are being completed and the deadlines met, offer them the freedom to work in whatever way is best for them right now.

When one of her employees died after a long illness, Debbie Maus discovered that because she was one of only two people working in the office, she had the space to process her loss. "There were days after Kelly died when I found myself frozen, just sitting here. I couldn't figure out what I needed to do next, even though I had lists and piles and plenty to do. But the fact that only one other person was here meant that I had the space to grieve without other members of my team constantly coming into my office."

**Enlist help.**
Ask your employee if it would be okay for a close colleague to check in and whether that person can share any concerns about what they're seeing. Encourage the point person to let you know if there's anything you might not be aware of (e.g., the griever is struggling with a project or finds it painful to be on the phone with clients) or notices anything worrisome (e.g., the griever seems withdrawn, repeatedly misses meetings, or stops taking care of themselves).

**Be patient.**
Your employee may not know what's difficult until they try it. They may need to sign off work early on hard days, their loved one's birthday, or the anniversary of their child's death. They may need encouragement or reassurance that their work is still up to your standards and help when it isn't. They may not be able to collaborate

with a coworker who ignores or diminishes their loss. They're suffering in ways you can't see, so be kind, no matter what.

### Take advance of technology.

Create a digital whiteboard, and ask everyone to post a note of support for your grieving colleague. Encourage the team to send cards via US mail since they can't express their condolences and concern in person. Allot time during your Zoom calls for people to check in or get to know each other better. Conduct an online survey before your next team meeting to get a sense of how everyone is doing. Meet once a month without an agenda so people can learn a new skill or have fun together.

Even after Andrea Corradini, Nike's global vice president of its Kids Footwear Division, moved her team meetings online during the pandemic, she continued their tradition of doing PechaKucha every Wednesday. Each week, three to five team members took turns displaying twenty slides about themselves and providing twenty seconds of commentary on each. One week after a teammate used his PechaKucha to share his love of reptiles and cars, he was killed drag racing one of his cars. One of Nike's artists made a digitally printed replica of the deceased employee's favorite car. The team set up a fund and created a company award in their colleague's honor. They rallied around his family.

Andrea believes that her team could not have come together in that way without having had to work remotely. "We had a hundred people at PechaKucha who got to learn about Gabe before he died. When we were gathering in person, it was like twelve people who could make the meeting. I've found so many silver linings in this whole situation. I hope we never go back to what it was like before. Even in grief support, it's been pretty magical just by the sheer number of people who can wrap warmth around another person."

# Grief and Compassion at Work

My employer and my academic discipline have gotten a lot more labor out of me because of the way they dealt with my husband's death. Organizations need to recognize employees as whole people. When losses happen, they need to express an ethic that you and your family come first. That they will be flexible about helping you through this. When you're treated that way, sure, it cultivates loyalty, but it also makes you want to give back because you feel like you are part of a community.

—Danilyn Rutherford

Every bereaved employee returns to work before they're ready. Although grief evolves and changes over time and eventually becomes easier to bear, the pain of losing one of our essential people never goes away. Like fingerprints, the process is unique to each of us. Just as there is no one right way to grieve, no two people's responses to a death, whether a similar type of loss or the same person, are identical.

Employees grappling with a devastating loss often feel split in two, as if they need to leave their grief-stricken self at home and bring only their polished, professional self to work. But living in two diametrically different worlds is exhausting and only makes people feel more lost and alone. Your goal should be to create a workplace where your colleagues can bring their whole selves—a culture where everyone strives to understand loss in general and how to support each team member's unique grief in particular.

It's tempting to focus on offering bereavement leave or a prescriptive plan when faced with a death in the workplace or a grieving employee, but being a brave leader and creating a compassionate culture will require more. You can be that leader who creates that culture by taking these actions:

- **Show up.** Acknowledge the loss. Attend the funeral or celebration of life. Send a card. Drop off a meal. Encourage your colleagues to do the same.
- **Honor everyone's pain.** The person who suffers the loss gets to say how significant it is. Your employee may have been raised by her grandmother. Her cousin may have been like a sister. His dog may have been his closest companion.
- **Say something.** Because so many people at work didn't acknowledge his sister's death, Marty Yee makes a point, when he knows a colleague's friend or family member has

died, to acknowledge the loss. He commented, "I just think it helps so much to do that."

- **Remain engaged.** Ask how you can help your grieving employee in the aftermath. What would help ease their return to work? What's going well? Where are they struggling? Seek out more than one perspective. If your team has lost a coworker, check in with multiple colleagues to get a variety of perspectives on how the team is doing and where you might need to do more. While Mark Ferdig was in Eritrea working as a program director for Mercy Corps, three of his employees were shot during an ambush, leaving two of them dead and the third paralyzed. Each employee was from a different ethnic group with different customs. Mark worked closely with those on his team who understood each tribe's traditions and customs on how to treat the bodies, how to support the grieving families, and the appropriate way to show respect. Mark said, "Whenever there's a crisis, culture wins every time. If you aren't open, if you come in with your own ego and don't adopt a learning position, you'll fail."
- **Remember that the smallest acts often mean the most.** An invitation to go for a cup of coffee or a walk, a note of encouragement, a hand on the shoulder, a quick "How are you doing today?" Providing a few hours off to attend a weekly support group. Acknowledging the birthday or death anniversary of the loved one who died. Christine Cosner recalled: "The chief financial officer showed up at my desk one morning with a small, clear plastic box that held notes from everyone in the company. She told me to pull one out when I needed a bit of encouragement. The notes said things like, 'Don't worry. You've got this, Chrissy.'"

- **Create a culture of compassion.** Support for a grieving employee should come from all levels of the organization from the CEO to the line staff. Although the employee's boss and their immediate coworkers will play the most active and important roles, senior leaders should also reach out to the grieving employee to offer condolences and their support. After Roger Harden's son died in an accident, the vice president of engine maintenance operations at Delta Air Lines called him at home to check on him. He checked on Roger again after he returned to work. When the senior vice president of technical operations learned about TJ's death during a site visit, he walked over to Roger, offered his condolences, and said, "If you need anything let me know." He began walking away, turned back, and said, "ANYTHING. If you need anything, call me. Delta or otherwise. Seriously."

- **Support your employee's choices, regardless of how you think you might act in a similar situation.** Some employees will need extra time off, while others may return to work right away. Some may want to talk about their loss, while others may want to act as if nothing has happened. Remind yourself that they are doing what's best for them.

- **Focus on the griever, but keep your eye on the team.** Your other employees will require coaching on how to support their grieving coworker, an understanding of why the griever needs the help they're receiving, and education on what to say and do to support the griever. You will overlook things and may make mistakes in support of your grieving employee. Your colleagues and other employees need to feel comfortable speaking up about their struggles, frustrations, and concerns, too.

- **Stay flexible.** Your employee's expectations may not match the reality of being back at work. Their needs will also change over time as they navigates and process their grief. As Mark Ferdig learned during a long career working internationally in challenging, often dangerous places, "there's no rule book on this stuff. So you adapt. The starting point is a place of compassion and empathy and being highly flexible based on the circumstances."

- **Be open to what grief can teach you.** You will learn how to forge stronger, more meaningful connections with your employees and colleagues and how to be more open, vulnerable, and brave. After her younger brother Chad died of a heart attack, high school teacher Janell Sowers Cinquini discovered that she was more willing to talk to her students about the hard things they were going through. "One of my students found his dad dead. I don't know all the circumstances. But he came to school after it happened because he didn't know where else to go. School was his safe place. During class, I knelt down next to his desk and said, 'I heard, and I'm so sorry.' Five years ago, before my brother died, I wouldn't have done that. I wouldn't have known that he wanted me to say something."
- **Understand that you can't outrun the grief.** As Trux Dole explains, "Grief is relentless, but it's going to come in waves. Allow it to be tidal. Be the kelp. Don't try to be the dock piling."
- **Be kind.**

Death makes us all awkward, yet it also compels us to grow and become more effective, empathetic leaders. Showing up for your employees on their hardest days is both the right thing to do and one of the best investments you can make in both the employee who's grieving and the rest of your team who's watching. The understanding and empathy you demonstrate will build a culture you can be proud of, one that will retain the best talent and inspire loyalty to your organization.

Grief is somewhere in every Zoom call and every meeting room, whether known or unknown, acknowledged or ignored. One employee may be mourning the death of a family member. Another may be missing a close coworker who's died or taken another job. Still another may be going through a divorce or serious illness. A grieving employee can, in time, return to a former level of productivity with a deepened respect, appreciation for, and loyalty to their organization, but only if they receive the support and acknowledgment they need during their worst days. So often what makes this possible is the small but important interactions that happen dozens of times a week between the bereaved employee and their manager and their coworkers—the unscripted opportunities to be supportive, to create space for the griever's feelings, and to ensure they have support. These are the moments that matter in a workplace.

# Sources Cited

Feldman, Amy. "How Hed Cycling's Anne Hed Picked Up the Pieces After the Death of Her Husband and Co-Founder." *Forbes*, November 10, 2016.

Gandhi, Vipula, and Jennifer Robison. "The 'Great Resignation' Is Really the 'Great Discontent.'" *Gallup at Work*, July 22, 2021.

*Grief Index: The Hidden Annual Costs of Grief in America's Workplace.* Grief Recovery Institute Educational Foundation, 2003.

Sinha, Vandana. "How I Faced a Tragic Loss at My Company." *Washington Business Journal*, April 14, 2015.

Smith, Sandy. "Phoning It In: Do You Know How Much Presenteeism Costs Your Business?" *EHS Today*, January 21, 2016. www.ehstoday.com/health/article/21918275/phoning -it-in-do-you-know-how-much-presenteeism-costs-your -business.

Sull, Donald, Charles Sull, and Ben Zweig. "Toxic Culture Is Driving the Great Resignation." *MIT Sloan Management Review*, January 22, 2022.

"2020 Workplace Safety Index: The Top 10 Causes of Disabling Injuries." Liberty Mutual Insurance. www.business .libertymutual.com/insights/2020-workplace-safety-index -the-top-10-causes-of-disabling-injuries. Accessed March 29, 2022.

*Using an Integrated Health and Safety Approach to Reduce Employee Presenteeism.* UL Health and Safety, 2015. www.legacy -uploads.ul.com/wp-content/uploads/sites/40/2015/12/ Integrated-Health-and-Safety-Approach.pdf.
Verdery, Ashton M., Emily Smith-Greenaway, Rachel Margolis, and Jonathan Daw. "Tracking the Reach of COVID-19 Kin Loss with a Bereavement Multiplier Applied to the United States." *Proceedings of the National Academy of Sciences* 117, no. 30 (2020): 17695–17701.

# Acknowledgments

Thank you to all the people who agreed to be interviewed for this
book:

Andrea Corradini, global vice president, Kids Footwear
Division, Nike

Anne Hed, CEO, Hed Cycling

Catherine Lemmon Kearney, consultant, California state
agency

Chopi DeRose, office manager, personal injury law firm

Christine Cosner, senior sales manager, PrintGlobe

Danilyn Rutherford, professor, University of Chicago, and
president, Wenner-Gren Foundation

Debbie Maus, executive director, nonprofit association

Janell Sowers Cinquini, history teacher, Lakeridge High
School, Lake Oswego, OR

Jim Crossen, president and general manager, American
subsidiary of a multinational corporation

Jody Nelsen, associate vice president for business affairs,
University of Texas at Dallas

Käthe Nathan, assistant to the regional vice president, Wells
Fargo Bank

Kelly Gallardo, senior managing consultant, Fortune 50 company

Linda Jellison, marketing specialist, homebuilding company

Linda Knight Crane, purchasing warehouse manager, Six Flags Great Adventure; customer service representative, Kohl's

Lisa Culp, executive director, Women's Empowerment, Sacramento, California

Lucy Dennis, ambassadors and campaigns officer, Cancer Research UK

Mark Ferdig, program director, Mercy Corps

Marty Yee, medical director, large technology company

Michelle Maghari, director of Visitor and Building Services, Crocker Art Museum, Sacramento, California

Rivkah Sass, library director and CEO, Sacramento Public Library

Roger Harden, lead repair design technician, Delta Tech Ops

Shari Roeseler, executive director, Society for the Blind, Sacramento, California

Tim Moye, manager, Delta Care and Scholarship Fund, Delta Air Lines

Trish Kelly, managing director, regional nonprofit

Trux Dole, senior e-business producer, Cambia Health Solutions

Appendix 1
# Resources

ONTARGET CONSULTING HELPS ORGANIZATIONS AND individuals act strategically, improve performance, and achieve their business goals. OnTarget works with leaders at all levels to create a more compassionate culture that recognizes and supports grief and loss of all kinds. Visit its resource page (ontargetconsulting.net/resources) to find seven downloadable PDFs providing practical advice on how to navigate all aspects of grief at work.

Salt Water (findyourharbor.com) is for those who have lost someone they can't live without—a child, sibling, parent, spouse, close friend, pet—and the people who love them. It provides a safe harbor where grievers can find comfort, support, and tools to survive their loss and rebuild their life in the aftermath.

## Articles and Books on Grief in the Workplace

Crowe, Kelsey, and Emily McDowell. *There Is No Good Card for This: What to Say and Do When Life Is Scary, Awful, and Unfair to People You Love.* New York: HarperOne, 2017.
"Current Practice and Data on Bereavement at Work." Marie Curie, 2021. www.mariecurie.org.uk/help/support/bereaved-family-friends/work/employer-resources/research-data-bereavement-work.

Dutton, Jane E., Peter J. Frost, Monica C. Worline, Jacoba M. Lilius, and Jason M. Kanov. "Leading in Times of Trauma." *Harvard Business Review*, January 2002.

"Employers Supporting Staff Through Bereavement." Sue Ryder, 2021. www.sueryder.org/how-we-can-help/bereavement -information/supporting-someone-else/employer -bereavement-support.

"How to Support a Grieving Colleague at Work." YouTube video, 2:04. Marie Curie, September 20, 2021. www.youtube.com /watch?v=HRIRLbbjrOA&t=38s.

McGuinness, Breffni. "Grief at Work: Developing a Bereavement Policy." Irish Hospice Foundation, 2007. www .hospicefoundation.ie/wp-content/uploads/2012/05/ GriefatWork.pdf.

McInerny, Nora. "Grieving Shouldn't Be a Privilege." *New York Times*, May 16, 2020.

Perreault, Yvette. "When Grief Comes to Work: Managing Grief and Loss in the Workplace." AIDS Bereavement and Resiliency Program of Ontario, 2011. www.catie.ca/sites/ default/files/When%20Grief%20Comes%20to%20Work_e .pdf.

Rodriguez, Jenny Calvert. "Employee Hardship Funds Help Companies Help Their People." *Harvard Business Review*, May 21, 2020.

## Organizations with Resources on Grief in the Workplace

Irish Hospice Foundation: hospicefoundation.ie.
Marie Curie: www.mariecurie.org.uk.
SuperFriend, an Australian organization, publishes three booklets on managing grief and loss in the workplace:

www.superfriend.com.au/resources/
managing-bereavement-grief-and-loss.

- "How to Support a Workplace Where There Is Grief
  or Loss."
- "Grief Is a Journey. Here's How You Can Work Your
  Way Through It."
- "Workmate Dealing with a Loss? Here's How You
  Can Help."

## Resources on Suicide Loss in the Workplace

Austin, Ciaran, and Breffni McGuinness. "Breaking the Silence
    in the Workplace: A Guide for Employers on Responding to
    Suicide in the Workplace." Irish Hospice Foundation, 2012.
    www.edepositireland.ie/handle/2262/83028.
McGuinness, Breffni, and Oliver Skehan. "Grief in the
    Workplace: Responding to Suicide." Irish Hospice
    Foundation, 2021. www.hospicefoundation.ie/our-supports
    -services/bereavement-loss-hub/grief-in-the-workplace
    /responding-to-suicide-a-guide-for-employers.

# *Appendix 2*
# Sample Bereavement Policy

The template below was provided by Marie Curie (www
.mariecurie.org.uk), the United Kingdom's leading end-of-life
charity.

## (YOUR ORGANISATION NAME) BEREAVEMENT POLICY

PURPOSE

1. It is important to be with, and support loved ones at the end
of life; to have time and space to grieve and make the necessary
arrangements following bereavement. Individual circumstances
vary and following bereavement we each respond differently to
grief and have different roles to play. That's why when supporting
loved ones at the end of life or grieving following a bereavement,
people should feel trusted and have the flexibility to respond.

OBJECTIVES

2. This policy describes our approach to bereavement and grief
at the end of life and sets out provisions for employees who lose
a loved one. It outlines circumstances in which the leave can be
granted and the support available to bereaved employees. (YOUR
ORGANISATON NAME) embraces flexible working and

encourages employees and their line managers to discuss how this flexibility can also support the employee whilst continuing to ensure organisational needs are met.

SCOPE

3. This policy applies to all employees of the organisation from the first day of their employment at **(YOUR ORGANISATON NAME)**, in accordance with the Equality Act 2010.

(**Important note:** references to employment law relate to England, Scotland, and Wales. It is essential that your policy references the law that applies in your country or if applicable a devolved nation within the United Kingdom e.g. Northern Ireland where different employment legislation is in place).

DEFINITIONS

4. Bereavement leave is time off for an employee to support loved ones nearing the end of their life, to grieve following bereavement or to deal with other matters relating to the death of loved ones and others.

5. Working week is the contractual weekly hours.

6. Day of bereavement leave:

- If you are a full-time employee, it is any working day.
- If you are a part-time employee, it is any working day you are contracted to work from your normal working pattern.
- If you are a variable hours worker, it is any day in the week you would have been due to work, and the entitlement will be pro-rata based on the average hours worked over the last 12 months before the leave request made.

## CONTRACTUAL STATUS

7. The policy does not include any terms and conditions of employment and is not contractual, and **(YOUR ORGANISATON NAME)** reserves the right to review and amend the policy as necessary.

## RELATED POLICIES

Flexible Working Policy

8. Below we outline additional circumstances in which **(YOUR ORGANISATON NAME)** would consider the provision of alternate or Bereavement Leave to be appropriate which may fall outside of the scope of the bereavement policy. For example, this could be a temporary leave of absence, longer term adjustments required to the working pattern to support the care of a dependant following an illness or death. This policy gives an indication as to whether this should be paid or unpaid. Line Managers should consider whether they are able to provide flexibility using our Flexible Working Policy and should use their discretion. HR should be consulted on matters where there is doubt or ambiguity.

## RESPONSIBILITIES

All employees will:

- Speak to their line manager and seek authorisation for bereavement leave as soon as possible.

Line managers will:

- Deal with requests for bereavement leave promptly and with empathy and compassion.
- Employees will be advised whether the time off will be paid or unpaid.

- Agree with the employee how to communicate their absence to the rest of the team.
- Ensure that adequate cover is arranged, where appropriate.
- Keep a record of all bereavement requests from members of their team.
- Remind employees taking Bereavement Leave that they can access support from **(INSERT RELEVANT SUPPORT FROM YOUR ORGANISATION).**

HR will:

- Update and monitor the policy to ensure consistency throughout the organisation.
- Provide support and guidance to employees and managers where required.

## TYPES OF BEREAVEMENT LEAVE
Bereavement for a loved one

9. Staff can ask for time off with pay to support and grieve for a loved one which can be a close or extended family member or friend.

10. Staff can apply for up to two working weeks' time off with pay for bereavement leave and can be extended to up to four working weeks' paid time off taking into account special circumstances, such as the distance to travel, religious rituals, responsibility for the funeral arrangements, responsibility for taking care of the estate of the lost one, and any matters that must be addressed when a loved one dies.

11. If more time is needed, then an application for a further two working weeks unpaid time off will be considered on a case-by-case basis.

12. We recognise that the impact of bereavement and the grief of loss can have an impact at different times for different people in

different circumstances. Time away can be taken flexibly either in a single day, in one block or in a combination, and is available for the period of up to 56 weeks after the death of a loved one.

13. This time can be used as follows:

- Supporting a loved one at the end of life; make care arrangements; spend some time with them to say goodbye and be with them at the time of death.
- Grieving following the death of a loved one; mourning, arranging, and attending the funeral or memorial service, resolving matters of inheritance, the fulfilment of family obligations, or managing estates.

Parental bereavement leave

(**Important note**: Statutory Bereavement Leave and payments for death of a child before they turn 18, or a stillbirth after 24 weeks of pregnancy came into effect for death on or after 6 April 2020. This applies across the UK with the exception of Northern Ireland. Review your policy regularly to ensure ongoing compliance with the law.)

14. Parental Bereavement Leave is a special type of leave to deal with the death of a child under the age of 18 or stillborn after 24 weeks' pregnancy. If this is statutory leave, this cannot be used at the same time as other statutory leave. Line managers/HR should ensure that employees are clear about their entitlements and how this may link in with bereavement leave.

15. The Parental Bereavement Leave can be taken by:

- birth parent (regardless of gender)
- adoptive parent (regardless of gender) if the child was living with them
- a person who lived with the child and had responsibility for them, for at least four weeks before they died

- 'intended parent'—due to become the legal parent through surrogacy (regardless of gender)
- partner of the child's parent, if they live with the child and the child's parent (regardless of gender) in an enduring family relationship

16. Eligible employees are normally entitled to take two working weeks paid leave, but this can be extended to up to four working weeks' paid time off taking into account special circumstances. If more time is needed, then an application for a further two working weeks unpaid time off will be considered on a case-by-case basis.

17. If more than one child dies, the employee is normally entitled to two working weeks of Parental Bereavement Leave for each child.

18. We recognise that the impact of bereavement and the grief of loss can have an impact at different times for different people in different circumstances. Time away can be taken flexibly either in a single day, in one block or in a combination, and is available for the period of up to 56 weeks after the death of a child. As above dependant on the situation this could impact with other forms of statutory leave. Line managers/HR should ensure that employees are clear about their entitlements and how this may link in with bereavement leave.

Paying respect

19. Time-off can also be given even where attendance is more about 'paying respect' or supporting others to attend funerals and memorials of loved ones, rather than because of the grief associated with death.

20. Normally, one day of paid leave would be agreed in these circumstances where absence is required for a full day. In the event that no leave allowance remains, unpaid leave may be used. Line

Managers can authorise an additional day in special circumstances, such as the distance to travel, religious rituals, or the individual's role in supporting others.

Pet or animal bereavement

21. For many of us, our pets or service animals (e.g. hearing dogs, guide dogs) are often seen as part of the family, so, when it comes to saying goodbye, it can be an extremely tough and emotional time. If you have lost, or are facing saying goodbye to, a loved pet or animal you should speak to your line manager. The animal's role would need to be considered: for example; working dog, service animal, or therapy animal.

22. **(YOUR ORGANISATON NAME)** will offer bereavement leave for your pets and animals. Normally it will be one day of paid or unpaid leave; however, each case will be reviewed individually.

Death of individuals with a connection to (INSERT ORGANISATION NAME) who are not employees

23. Many employees are likely to have had an ongoing professional relationship with **(ADAPT FOR YOUR ORGANISATION** e.g. suppliers, service users etc). Our presence at a funeral or memorial service is always noted. **(YOUR ORGANISATON NAME)** would normally enable you to take paid-time-off during working hours to attend a funeral or memorial service and allow you to pay your respects, before returning to work. Paid leave is an option if required.

24. It should always be decided on a case by case basis, and all requests need to be discussed with the line managers who will decide. Their decision will be based on the current workload, the time needed for travel and personal circumstances. None of our staff should feel pressure to attend the funeral or memorial and the

decision to attend or not to attend the funeral/memorial/service should be made by the individual, considering their wellbeing and work-life balance.

## MANAGING BEREAVEMENT LEAVE
### Approving bereavement leave

25. Line managers have the discretion to approve paid and unpaid bereavement leave (outside of any statutory requirements referenced above). Line managers will work with employees on a case-by-case basis to determine what the employee's needs are and what **(YOUR ORGANISATON NAME)** is able to offer.

### Communication to the team

26. It is a bereaved employee's right to decide how much information they want co-workers to know, and if they wish to be contacted by colleagues. This should be discussed with the line manager.

### Annual Leave during bereavement leave

27. An employee who suffers a bereavement while on annual leave may have the opportunity to pause their annual leave to be placed on bereavement leave. This would allow their annual leave to be rescheduled for a future date. It is recommended that the employees contact the line manager as soon as possible to discuss more fully the circumstances.

### Return to work after bereavement leave

28. Employees returning to work from bereavement leave can come back on their normal working arrangements or with agreement for a phased return. Sometimes a full return to work may not be possible immediately after the death of a close person, for example, when the grief is likely to impact their ability to perform their role, or where new child care arrangements have to be sourced, or

responsibility for the care of an elderly parent has transferred to the employee. **(YOUR ORGANISATON NAME)** is open to flexible working and in such instances will allow a phased return to work on a part-time or reduced hours basis for an agreed period of time if viable. Alternative duties may also be considered. Any change will need to be discussed and approved by the line manager and will be managed in line with the flexible working policy.

Adjustment to work

29. An employee with any concerns about the grieving process impacting on their work performance should discuss this in confidence with either their line manager or the Human Resources Department, to ensure that any reasonable adjustments that may be necessary are discussed and put in place and that the employee is supported in their return to the full range of duties and responsibilities that they had prior to the bereavement or their duties and responsibilities are adjusted (as necessary) with the prior agreement of line manager.

30. **(YOUR ORGANISATON NAME)** is aware that grief can cause depression, which may be considered a disability. **(YOUR ORGANISATON NAME)** will ensure that employees with a disability are not subject to discrimination. Consideration will be given to whether there are reasonable adjustments that could be made to the requirements to a job or other aspects of working arrangements that will provide support at work and assist a return to work. **(YOUR ORGANISATON NAME)** may ask employees to speak to the occupational health service for advice on how best to manage any impacts on work.

OTHER SUPPORT FOR BEREAVEMENT

**Note:** include the support that is available for your staff. For example, at Marie Curie, we provide:

Counselling services
Via our Employee Assistance Programme, Marie Curie provides staff with a free and completely confidential counselling service which operates 24 hours a day, 365 days a year. Staff can call the service for any issue which may be impacting on their work or personal lives, including bereavement. Face to face counselling can also be arranged.

Financial support
There are many ways staff can get help with funeral costs. If employees don't qualify for the Government's 'Funeral Payments' scheme or for the Bereavement Payment, then they can ask Marie Curie for a loan to help with the funeral cost. The cost will be deducted from salary over an agreed period up to a maximum of 12 months.

Marie Curie Information and Support
Our colleagues are also encouraged to access Marie Curie's services which offers help with practical information and support on all aspects of life with terminal illness, dying and bereavement.

*(September 2021)*

# Two Models of Workplace Grief Support

**Wrenched Hearts** is a peer support group for Delta Air Lines employees who have lost a child, and at this writing it's the only program of its kind in corporate America. Conceived by Delta Air Lines employee Tim Moye after the death of his son Jason in 2011, the group began in Tech Ops, where Tim worked at the time. He explained, "We're all a bunch of gear heads, and what we've been through is heart wrenching."

Since its launch on the two-year anniversary of Jason's death on February 5, 2013, the group has grown from thirty-five people to almost three hundred company-wide. Membership is open to any of Delta's eighty thousand employees, and meetings are held in multiple locations across the United States.

To learn more, watch Tim's TED talk, "Legacy from Loss" (www .youtube.com/watch?v=ZlYRFpzy4c8), or contact him directly at Tim.Moye@delta.com.

**Grief and Bereavement Wellbeing Network** at Cancer Research UK provides a safe and inclusive environment for Cancer Research's employees to support all types of grief, from ambiguous loss and anticipatory grief to grief support following a bereavement, from day one to decades later.

In addition to bringing employees and managers together for peer support, the Network also champions internal policy change to create a compassionate workplace.

Launched in March 2021 by Lucy Dennis after the death of her father, the Network started with coffee mornings once a month, hosted by Lucy, where she invited other grieving employees to come and talk about their grief. As the group and the interest grew, Lucy recruited eight more volunteers to work with her on a strategy to expand the Network's offerings, which now include:

- quarterly guest speakers
- special events held around certain holidays like Mother's Day, Father's Day, National Siblings Day, and so on
- a support group on fertility and baby loss that meets separately and is run by those employees who have experience with baby loss, miscarriage, and infertility
- a newsletter with relevant news articles, guest blog posts, resources, and information about external events

The Network's chairpersons of learning and development are building a grief wellness action plan for bereaved employees in which they can share the most important dates for them (their loved one's date of death and birthday, their anniversary, any days that could be triggering for them) as well as a list of what they've been struggling with since returning to work, how they want to be communicated with about their grief, what kind of support they need on a bad day, and so on.

The Network's policy chairs are working on consolidating all of Cancer Research UK's workplace policies that could be part of a compassionate policy so that employees will know about and be able to use any that are applicable when a loved one is dying or has died. The policy chairs are also creating case studies, drawn from real life examples, of good and poor practices around compassionate leave, which they plan to turn into a policy guidance document. The goal is to educate managers about best practices.

To learn more, contact Lucy Dennis via LinkedIn at www .linkedin.com/in/lucy-dennis-75386b199.

www.ingramcontent.com/pod-product-compliance
Lightning Source LLC
Chambersburg PA
CBHW051440150726
48000CB00005B/2183